DATE DUE

JAN 2 9 2009	

LOST GOSPELS & HIDDEN CODES
New Concepts of Scripture

RELIGION & MODERN CULTURE
Title List

LOST GOSPELS & HIDDEN CODES
New Concepts of Scripture

by Kenneth McIntosh, M.Div.

Mason Crest Publishers
Philadelphia

Mason Crest Publishers Inc.
370 Reed Road
Broomall, Pennsylvania 19008
(866) MCP-BOOK (toll free)

First printing
1 2 3 4 5 6 7 8 9 10

Library of Congress Cataloging-in-Publication Data

McIntosh, Kenneth, 1959-
  Lost Gospels and hidden codes : new concepts of Scripture / by Kenneth R.
McIntosh.
     p. cm. — (Religion and modern culture)
  Includes bibliographical references and index.
  ISBN 1-59084-982-5   ISBN 1-59084-970-1 (series)
  1. Apocryphal Gospels. 2. Christianity--Origin. I. Title. II. Series.
  BS2851.M35 2006
  229'.8—dc22
                                    2005012957

Produced by Harding House Publishing Service, Inc.
www.hardinghousepages.com
Interior design by Dianne Hodack.
Cover design by MK Bassett-Harvey.
Printed in India.

CONTENTS

INTRODUCTION

by Dr. Marcus J. Borg

You are about to begin an important and exciting experience: the study of modern religion. Knowing about religion—and religions—is vital for understanding our neighbors, whether they live down the street or across the globe.

Despite the modern trend toward religious doubt, most of the world's population continues to be religious. Of the approximately six billion people alive today, around two billion are Christians, one billion are Muslims, 800 million are Hindus, and 400 million are Buddhists. Smaller numbers are Sikhs, Shinto, Confucian, Taoist, Jewish, and indigenous religions.

Religion plays an especially important role in North America. The United States is the most religious country in the Western world: about 80 percent of Americans say that religion is "important" or "very important" to them. Around 95 percent say they believe in God. These figures are very different in Europe, where the percentages are much smaller. Canada is "in between": the figures are lower than for the United States, but significantly higher than in Europe. In Canada, 68 percent of citizens say religion is of "high importance," and 81 percent believe in God or a higher being.

The United States is largely Christian. Around 80 percent describe themselves as Christian. In Canada, professing Christians are 77 percent of the population. But religious diversity is growing. According to Harvard scholar Diana Eck's recent book *A New Religious America*, the United States has recently become the most religiously diverse country in the world. Canada is also a country of great religious variety.

Fifty years ago, religious diversity in the United States meant Protestants, Catholics, and Jews, but since the 1960s, immigration from Asia, the Middle East, and Africa has dramatically increased the number of people practicing other religions. There are now about six million Muslims, four million Buddhists, and a million Hindus in the United States. To compare these figures to two historically important Protestant denominations in the United States, about 3.5 million are Presbyterians and 2.5 million are Episcopalians. There are more Buddhists in the United States than either of these denominations, and as many Muslims as the two denominations combined. This means that knowing about other religions is not just knowing about people in other parts of the world—but about knowing people in our schools, workplaces, and neighborhoods.

Moreover, religious diversity does not simply exist between religions. It is found within Christianity itself:

- There are many different forms of Christian worship. They range from Quaker silence to contemporary worship with rock music to traditional liturgical worship among Catholics and Episcopalians to Pentecostal enthusiasm and speaking in tongues.

- Christians are divided about the importance of an afterlife. For some, the next life—a paradise beyond death—is their primary motive for being Christian. For other Christians, the afterlife does not matter nearly as much. Instead, a relationship with God that transforms our lives this side of death is the primary motive.
- Christians are divided about the Bible. Some are biblical literalists who believe that the Bible is to be interpreted literally and factually as the inerrant revelation of God, true in every respect and true for all time. Other Christians understand the Bible more symbolically as the witness of two ancient communities—biblical Israel and early Christianity—to their life with God.

Christians are also divided about the role of religion in public life. Some understand "separation of church and state" to mean "separation of religion and politics." Other Christians seek to bring Christian values into public life. Some (commonly called "the Christian Right") are concerned with public policy issues such as abortion, prayer in schools, marriage as only heterosexual, and pornography. Still other Christians name the central public policy issues as American imperialism, war, economic injustice, racism, health care, and so forth. For the first group, values are primarily concerned with individual behavior. For the second group, values are also concerned with group behavior and social systems. The study of religion in North America involves not only becoming aware of other religions but also becoming aware of differences within Christianity itself. Such study can help us to understand people with different convictions and practices.

And there is one more reason why such study is important and exciting: religions deal with the largest questions of life. These questions are intellectual, moral, and personal. Most centrally, they are:

- What is real? The religions of the world agree that "the real" is more than the space-time world of matter and energy.
- How then shall we live?
- How can we be "in touch" with "the real"? How can we connect with it and become more deeply centered in it?

This series will put you in touch with other ways of seeing reality and how to live.

Chapter 1

RELIGION & MODERN CULTURE

DIVINE WORDS

American Professor Robert Langdon and French code expert Sophie Neveu are running for their lives. They have stumbled onto an ancient mystery—and their only clues are hidden in the paintings by the famous artist, Leonardo da Vinci. Someone has already murdered the curator of the Louvre museum in Paris to keep these clues hidden, and now the French police are pursuing Langdon on false murder charges. Meanwhile, a psychopathic priest working for the Catholic Church is trying to murder them. Now, Langdon and Neveu are hiding in the home of Leigh Teabing, an expert on the **Holy Grail** and other ancient matters.

The pair asks Teabing for information about the mystery. To answer their questions, "Teabing located a huge book and pulled it toward them across the table. The leather-bound edition was poster-sized, like a huge atlas. The cover read: *The Gnostic gospels.* . . . 'These are photocopies of the Nag Hammadi and Dead Sea Scrolls, which I mentioned earlier,' Teabing said. 'The earliest Christian records. Troublingly, they do not match up with the gospels in the Bible.'"

Teabing goes on to read a passage from *The Gospel of Philip*, which, he explains, suggests a sexual relationship between Jesus Christ and Mary Magdalene. He suggests the Catholic Church hid these ancient records, favoring the "official" gospels contained in the Bible. He says the Church did so in order to convince people Jesus was divine—and in so doing, increase the Church's influence.

These events take place in *The Da Vinci Code* by Dan Brown. The book has sold more than 17 million copies and set the record for adult novel sales in a single year. The movie based on the same story is sure to make the book even more popular.

Dan Brown's book is certainly fascinating reading and a good action story. Janet Maslin of the *New York Times* called it a "riddle-filled, code-breaking, exhilaratingly brainy thriller." Patrick Anderson of the *Washington Post* says *The Da Vinci Code* is "a theological thriller that is both fascinating and fun."

At the same time, many readers wonder, "Could the claims in this book be true? Was Jesus married? Has the Catholic Church hidden the real Jesus from the world for almost two thousand years?"

Dan Brown suggests his novel is more than just fiction. The first page states, "All descriptions of artwork, architecture, documents, and secret rituals in this novel are accurate." However, historians and experts on ancient documents dismiss his claims. Nevertheless, *The Da Vinci Code* has proven popular with the American public—and controversial as well. As Amy Bernstein points out in *U.S. News & World Report Secrets of* The Da Vinci Code, "The book is very disturbing to

GLOSSARY

Gnostic Gospels: Writings of an early Christian group known as the Gnostics that were not included in the New Testament.

Holy Grail: According to some, the cup used by Jesus at the Last Supper, and by Joseph of Arimathea to catch Jesus's blood at the crucifixion.

liberal: Tolerant of different views and standards of behavior in others.

many because Dan Brown is . . . attacking the foundations of Christianity, and in particular the divinity of Christ."

A character in *The Da Vinci Code* says documents more ancient than the Christian Bible reveal hidden truths about Jesus. Curiously, Dan Brown does not devalue the idea of scripture itself. Instead, he replaces traditional Christian scriptures—the New Testament gospels—with another form of scripture, the ***Gnostic Gospels***.

"Thy word is a lamp to my feet and a light to my path."

—Psalm 119:105

WHAT IS SCRIPTURE, & WHY IS IT IMPORTANT?

The most important beliefs of Christians come from scripture, especially the Gospels found in the New Testament. According to Lee M. McDonald, principal of the college and professor of New Testament studies at Acadia Divinity College in Nova Scotia, Canada, "Among the world's great religions, Judaism, Christianity, and Islam have defined themselves in terms of a sacred written text."

Since people of faith regard scriptures as divine, they also believe these sacred writings have power to say how people should behave. Interpretations of sacred scripture have influenced most of the important social issues in North America over the past decades—the care of the poor, preventing warfare, sexual behavior, civil rights, and so on. Thus, questions concerning scripture become important for all members living in a society, whether or not they share beliefs in these scriptures.

CHRISTIAN VIEWS OF SCRIPTURE

In his church, a preacher reads aloud from the Bible: "In Philippians 4:13, the Apostle Paul promises believers, 'I can do all things through Christ who strengthens me.'" The preacher pauses a moment to let his congregation reflect on the words. Then he continues: "That means, if we allow sinful or bad habits to continue in our lives, it is because we choose to do so. God has promised power to deliver us, if we will only believe in his word."

"How can young people keep their way pure? By living according to your word."

—*Psalm 119:9*

The pastor pauses again, only this time not for the sake of his audience. A thought has just hit him. The pastor is speaking aloud—but he is speaking to himself as much as to the church. "That means I *can* quit smoking—right away." He looks again at his congregation, and at his wife sitting with them. "I'm going to quit smoking, today!"

And he does quit, just like that. Like innumerable Christians before him, this man finds strength to change his life by believing in the Bible.

The United States and Canada may be the most diverse countries on earth in terms of religion—but Christianity remains the most influential religious belief, especially in the United States, where more than three out of four citizens define themselves as "Christian." And the Bible is vital to Christian faith. Late in the life of German theologian Karl Barth, perhaps the most important Christian thinker of the past century, a reporter asked him to sum up his religious beliefs. In answer, the brilliant theologian quoted a children's ditty: "Jesus loves me this I know, for the Bible tells me so."

Christians in the twenty-first century understand the Bible in a variety of ways. According to the Catechism of the Catholic Church, Catholics regard the Bible "not as a human word, but as what it really is, the Word of God." At the same time, "In Sacred Scripture, God speaks to man in a human way . . . the reader must take into account the conditions of their time and culture." How can believers tell which parts of the Bible are God's word for today and which parts were for people in ancient culture? The *Catechism* says, "Sacred Scripture is written principally in the church's heart rather in the documents and records, for the Church carries in her Tradition the living memorial of God's word." In other words, the teachings of the Church help Catholics to interpret the Bible.

THE MEANING OF SCRIPTURE

People of faith regard their scriptures as uniquely superior to other writings. What does it mean to say that the Bible or the Qur'an is scripture? According to Lee M. McDonald, "scriptures":

1. are written collections

2. are from God

3. communicate God's will

4. function forever in guiding people's lives.

Believers in so-called mainstream churches—such as United Methodist, Episcopal, Presbyterian, and United Church of Christ—often hold a more *liberal* view of the Bible. In his book *The Heart of Christianity*, professor of religion Marcus Borg explains this view: "Christianity is centered in the Bible . . . God is also known in other ways and other religions, I am convinced, but to be a Christian is to be centered in the God of the Bible." He goes on to list various claims of the Bible that people in the twenty-first century find offensive or incredible. Considering these concerns, Professor Borg believes "the Bible is not absolute truth." Modern readers must interpret the Bible in light of science and historical study. Nonetheless, the stories of the Bible "shape our sense of who we are and what our life with God is about."

In the United States, evangelical Christians are highly influential. In contrast to Roman Catholics, evangelicals usually do not regard church traditions or teachings as equal in authority with the Bible. They say, "Scripture alone is the final authority on church matters." At the same time, evangelicals sometimes disagree among themselves regarding how much of the Bible is literal truth. Those who hold to the doctrine of inerrancy believe that the Bible is without error of any kind: "It is without error in all matters it addresses, including history and even science." Others believe the Bible is literally true in matters of faith and practice, though not necessarily in matters of science or history.

The statements above are generalizations. Many Christians avoid labels that pigeonhole their views of the Bible. In all Christian traditions, however, the Bible is important.

Christians adopted their Old Testament from Judaism. In Judaism, as in Christianity, there is a variety of different understandings regarding the nature of the Bible. Likewise, the Jewish scriptures are essential to all forms of Jewish faith.

MODERN ALTERNATIVES
TO TRADITIONAL SCRIPTURES

Today, North Americans continue to value scripture. However, some define scripture in new ways. They ask whether the "Lost Gospels" can claim equal authority with the New Testament Gospels. The Nag Hammadi Library, discovered in 1945 in Egypt, contains books with titles like *The Gospel of Thomas*, *The Gospel of Philip*, and *The Apocalypse of Peter*. These books describe a form of Christianity different from that described in the New Testament: Gnosticism, the belief that Jesus imparted secret knowledge to certain special followers, knowledge not known by the writers of the Bible.

While some people are considering new scriptures, others find hidden meanings in the Bible. In 1997, *The Bible Code*, written by journalist Michael Drosnin, made the bestseller lists for months. It claims the Hebrew Bible contains a very complex code that reveals events that took place thousands of years after the Bible was written.

The Da Vinci Code suggests yet another source of religious authority. The novel's author hints that secret societies have guarded religious truths through the ages. These secret societies include the Cathars (a medieval cult with beliefs similar to Gnosticism), the Knights Templar (warrior monks who guarded Jerusalem in the Middle Ages), and the Priory of Sion (an alleged French secret society).

Clearly, the concept of scripture and divine authority is often complicated, and people have different views on these topics. Not everyone understands how Jews and Christians decided God inspired their Bibles in the first place. Others wonder why, for example, they picked the Gospel of Mark, and not the Gospel of Mary Magdalene, for inclusion in the Bible.

DIVINE WORDS

Chapter 2

DISCERNING THE WORD OF THE LORD

Soldiers pounded on the door. "Open up. We command you in the name of the Emperor!"

Father Athelios prayed a quick silent prayer: *Dear Lord, have mercy on my poor soul.* He walked to the entrance and opened the door.

Four tall Romans in shining metal armor swept into the room. Their swords were drawn as they glared at the little priest. The officer in charge growled, "You know why we are here?"

Father Athelios bowed a little to show respect. "Our Emperor Diocletian has commanded that we turn over all of our sacred writings to be publicly burned."

The officer nodded. "You Christians worship Jesus as if he was your lord. Only the emperor is lord! Your writings threaten to divide our glorious empire. Do you know what will happen to you, Priest Athelios, if you do not hand over your sacred writings?"

Father Athelios replied quietly, "If I refuse our emperor's order, I will be jailed—perhaps I will be tortured or executed. I fear and obey our emperor, so you men shall have no problems. The sacred writings are in my study—back there." He pointed to a door that led into a small room behind the church sanctuary. "You may take them."

"Men," the officer ordered, "search this church. Make sure all the books are in that room. If this little man has lied to us, gut him like a fish." The other three soldiers ran to do his bidding.

Father Athelios stood quietly before the officer, waiting. On the outside, he appeared calm. On the inside, he was silently praying. *Christ protect me and protect your Holy Word.*

The priest alone knew the desperate decision he had made earlier that day. Father Athelios expected the soldiers would come. All night he prayed, asking God how he should respond to the emperor's orders. In the Gospel, Jesus commanded, "Give to Caesar what is Caesar's." But Jesus also said, "Do not throw pearls before pigs"—and in Father Athelios's mind, that meant, "Don't let the pagans destroy God's Word." How could the priest obey both commands?

As the morning sun had lit the sky, a solution came into Father Athelios's head. It seemed the answer to his prayers. He would give the soldiers sacred writings—or rather what some Christians believed were sacred writings! After all, some people regarded the *Shepherd of Hermas*, the *Epistle of Barnabas*, the *Didache*, and the *Revelation of Peter* as Holy Scripture. Other Christians, including Father Athelios, recognized only the four Gospels of Matthew, Mark, Luke, and John, along with the letters of Saint Paul.

Neatly stacked on the priest's desk were the four questionable books, waiting for the soldiers. Father Athelios reminded himself, *I have not lied to the soldiers—some Christians regard these books as sacred writing.* He had hidden a thick leather book containing the four Gospels underneath a haystack behind the church, and he had secreted another book containing Paul's letters beneath the gilded altar.

GLOSSARY

primary sources: Eyewitnesses to an event.

Father Athelios accomplished three important things that day. First, he saved his own life. Second, he preserved what he regarded as the words of God, hiding scripture for later generations. Third, he chose which books should—and which books should not—be included as part of the Bible.

Father Athelios is a fictional character, but the story is historically accurate. In the year 303, Emperor Diocletian decreed Christian scriptures be destroyed throughout the empire. Countless priests—nameless to us today—made choices just like Father Athelios did. They surrendered books they thought were dubious in terms of divine inspiration and hid books they regarded as God's true Word. The choices made by these clergy in the fourth century helped shape what Christians regard as the New Testament today.

THE JEWISH CANON

The Bible is a collection of books gathered under one cover. The collection of books that make up the Bible is the canon, a Greek word meaning "measurement." In a long process that took centuries to complete, Jewish and Christian leaders decided how to "measure" the Bible. They chose which books were and were not divinely inspired.

Before the sixth century BCE, Jews depended on small collections of sacred writing that showed them how to live according to God's desires. These included the Ten Commandments, which would later serve as a moral basis for Western civilization. Over time, Jewish scribes put the collected writings together into the Torah, the five books of Moses.

In 587 BCE, Jews experienced a crisis. Babylon captured and burned the holy city Jerusalem, enslaving the Jewish nation. Seventy years later, Babylon rulers allowed some Jews to return to their own land. These returning exiles asked themselves why God allowed such awful things to happen. They concluded they had not been living according to God's wishes. A priest, Ezra, decided that in order to know God's will, the Jews would have to know and understand the Torah. According to the Book of Nehemiah, he ordered all the people to gather, while he stood above them in a tower and delivered history's first Bible sermon. From this point, Judaism became a religion based on scripture.

Around 200 BCE, Jewish priests added to the Bible writings they called the Prophets. These include Isaiah, Jeremiah, and Ezekiel. The priests also included books of history and the Psalms. Four centuries later (200 CE), Jewish rabbis felt the Bible needed closure. However, they disagreed regarding the number of books in the canon. Jews living in the Holy Land believed the books that make up the Hebrew Bible today were the complete Bible. Other Jews wanted seven more books in their canon: Tobit, Judith, Baruch, Sirach, Wisdom, and 1 and 2 Maccabees.

Around this time, Christians also accepted the Jewish canon as their Old Testament. Since the Jews were in disagreement over the books of their Bible, the Christian church inherited the same issues. Shortly afterward, Jews agreed to adopt the shorter list. Christians, however, were unable to agree on a list. Catholics and Protestants still disagree regarding the number of books in the Old Testament.

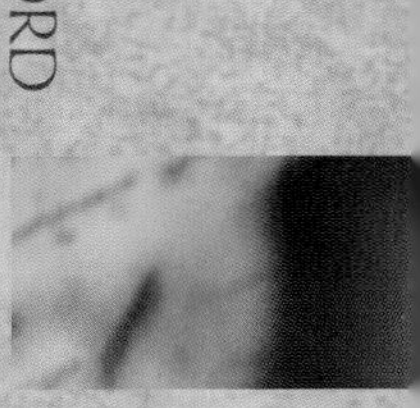

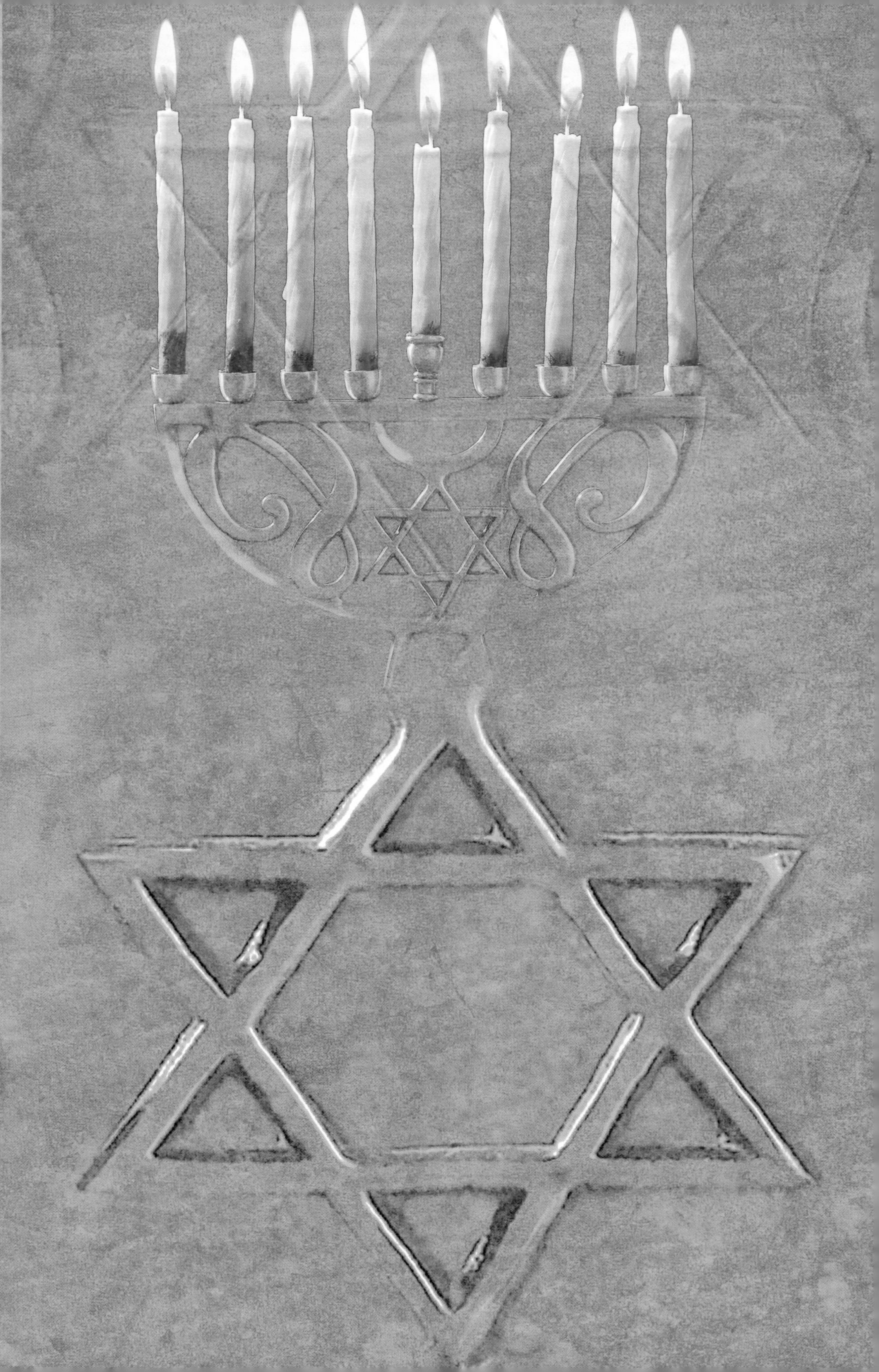

"All Scripture is inspired by God."
  —*2 Timothy 3:16*

HOW THE NEW TESTAMENT WAS WRITTEN

The earliest Christians centered their faith on a person, Jesus, rather than a book. During the years that Jesus taught, his students committed his sayings to memory. Approximately twenty years after Jesus's death, Paul of Tarsus began writing letters to Jesus's followers in cities around the Roman Empire.

Paul was a rabbi who had previously persecuted Christians. After a dramatic conversion, he became a leader in the Christian community. Paul's letters are the first Christian writings. Some scholars question whether Paul actually wrote the Bible books titled Ephesians, Colossians, and 1 and 2 Timothy. All agree, however, that Paul wrote Romans, 1 and 2 Corinthians, Galatians, and Philippians. These books prove that within decades of Jesus's lifetime, Christians worshipped Jesus as God.

For decades, Christians passed on the teachings of Christ by word of mouth. However, as the people who knew Jesus personally became elderly, some believers wanted a written record of his life. Around 70 CE, John Mark wrote the first Gospel—the Gospel of Mark. Mark wrote the story as the Apostle Peter told it to him.

The word "gospel" is not actually a religious term; it means simply "good news." In the ancient world, Greek and Roman writers composed many books proclaiming the "good news" about emperors and kings whose actions benefited their subjects. The New Testament Gospels tell the good news of how King Jesus blessed his followers. The Gospels contain history, but the Gospel writers relate history primarily according to their religious purpose.

DATING SYSTEMS & THEIR MEANING

You might be accustomed to seeing dates expressed with the abbreviations BC or AD, as in the year 1000 BC or the year AD 1900. For centuries, this dating system has been the most common in the Western world. However, since BC and AD are based on Christianity (BC stands for Before Christ and AD stands for *anno Domini*, Latin for "in the year of our Lord"), many people now prefer to use abbreviations that people from all religions can be comfortable using. The abbreviations BCE (meaning Before Common Era) and CE (meaning Common Era) mark time in the same way (for example, 1000 BC is the same year as 1000 BCE, and AD 1900 is the same year as 1900 CE), but BCE and CE do not have the same religious overtones as BC and AD.

Around 80 to 90 CE, the Gospel we call Matthew was composed for Jewish readers. The author wrote his book using the Gospel of Mark and a spoken tradition of Jesus's sayings. He also included numerous quotes from the Hebrew Bible to support his conviction that Jesus was the Christ predicted by Israel's ancient prophets.

About the same time, Luke, a doctor friend of the Apostle Paul, wrote his Gospel for a Greek and Roman audience. Using sources similar to those used by Matthew, Luke emphasized Jesus's concern for the poor. He wanted non-Jewish readers to understand that Jesus intended his message for all cultures.

Another decade later (90–100 CE), someone known as "the beloved disciple" wrote the Gospel of John. Some Christians believe John the son of Zebedee was the author, while other scholars question that. This Gospel is so different from the other three that some Bible professors question whether John contains actual sayings of Jesus or interpretations and summaries of what Jesus said. However, parts of the Gospel of John appear to be eyewitness accounts.

DEFINING THE CHRISTIAN BIBLE

In his novel *The Da Vinci Code*, Dan Brown claims, "The Bible as we know it today, was collated by the Roman emperor Constantine the great." Most scholars, however, would disagree with the novelist on this point. For more than a century before Constantine, Christians had been selecting their canon. The Diocletian persecution had already helped define the New Testament (see the beginning of this chapter). Constantine did order scribes to produce Bibles for each city in the empire. However, the emperor gave no orders regarding the contents of those Bibles.

The Da Vinci Code also claims that Constantine influenced one of the central themes of the New Testament. Speaking about the Council of Nicaea, which was held by Constantine in the fourth century, the character Leigh Teabing says, "until that moment in history, Jesus was viewed by his followers as a mortal prophet . . . a great and powerful man, but a man nevertheless. A mortal." Sophie asks, "Not the Son of God?" and Teabing replies, "Right, Jesus' establishment as 'the Son of God' was officially proposed and voted on by the Council of Nicaea."

COUNTING THE BOOKS OF THE BIBLE

Jews count twenty-four books in Hebrew scripture—what Christians often refer to as the Old Testament. Although the number is different, the content of these twenty-four books is identical to the thirty-nine books of the Protestant Old Testament. Jewish Bibles place twelve prophetic books together as one, and count "two-part" books as one (in other words, 1 and 2 Kings is considered one book). Catholics count forty-six books of the Old Testament and twenty-seven in the New Testament, for a total of seventy-three books in the Bible. Protestants count thirty-nine books in the Old Testament and twenty-seven in the New Testament, for a total of sixty-six books in the Bible. The Greek Orthodox Church adds five more books to the Old Testament, adding up to seventy-eight. The Coptic Church of Ethiopia takes the prize for the most books; their Bible has a grand total of eighty-one books.

This statement from the novel is pure fiction. In fact, Christians claimed Jesus was divine almost three centuries before Constantine. The New Testament book of Philippians, written around 50 CE, says Christ "was in very nature God." The Gnostics, whom Leigh Teabing claims were the earliest and most authentic Christians, all worshipped Jesus as divine. Delegates at the Council of Nicaea debated whether "Son of God" made Jesus equal with God the Father, or a lesser sort of deity. No one at the council regarded Christ as a mere mortal.

The first record of a New Testament identical to the modern twenty-seven books comes in the year 367. Athanasius, the bishop of Alexandria, Egypt, wrote a letter to all the churches, listing the books that the Christian church accepted as divinely inspired. From that time forward, the majority of believers in Christ used the same New Testament they do today.

The Old Testament canon, however, remained uncertain until a radical young monk named Martin Luther split the Christian church into its Protestant and Catholic halves in the sixteenth century. Luther declared the Old Testament to include only thirty-nine books. The Catholic Church responded by declaring that forty-six books were divinely inspired. Catholics and Protestants have had two different Old Testaments ever since.

THE LOST BOOKS & ALMOST-LOST BOOKS OF THE BIBLE

Christians were not unanimous in their choices of Bible books. Many believers especially wanted to see two books included in the New Testament, but church leaders ultimately denied them. One popular book was the *Didache*, written by an anonymous Christian between 90 and 100 CE, a book of instruction in Christian practices and beliefs. Another "almost-made-it" book of the Bible was the *Shepherd of Hermas*, in which Hermas records a series of visions, each of which command the listener to live a strict religious life.

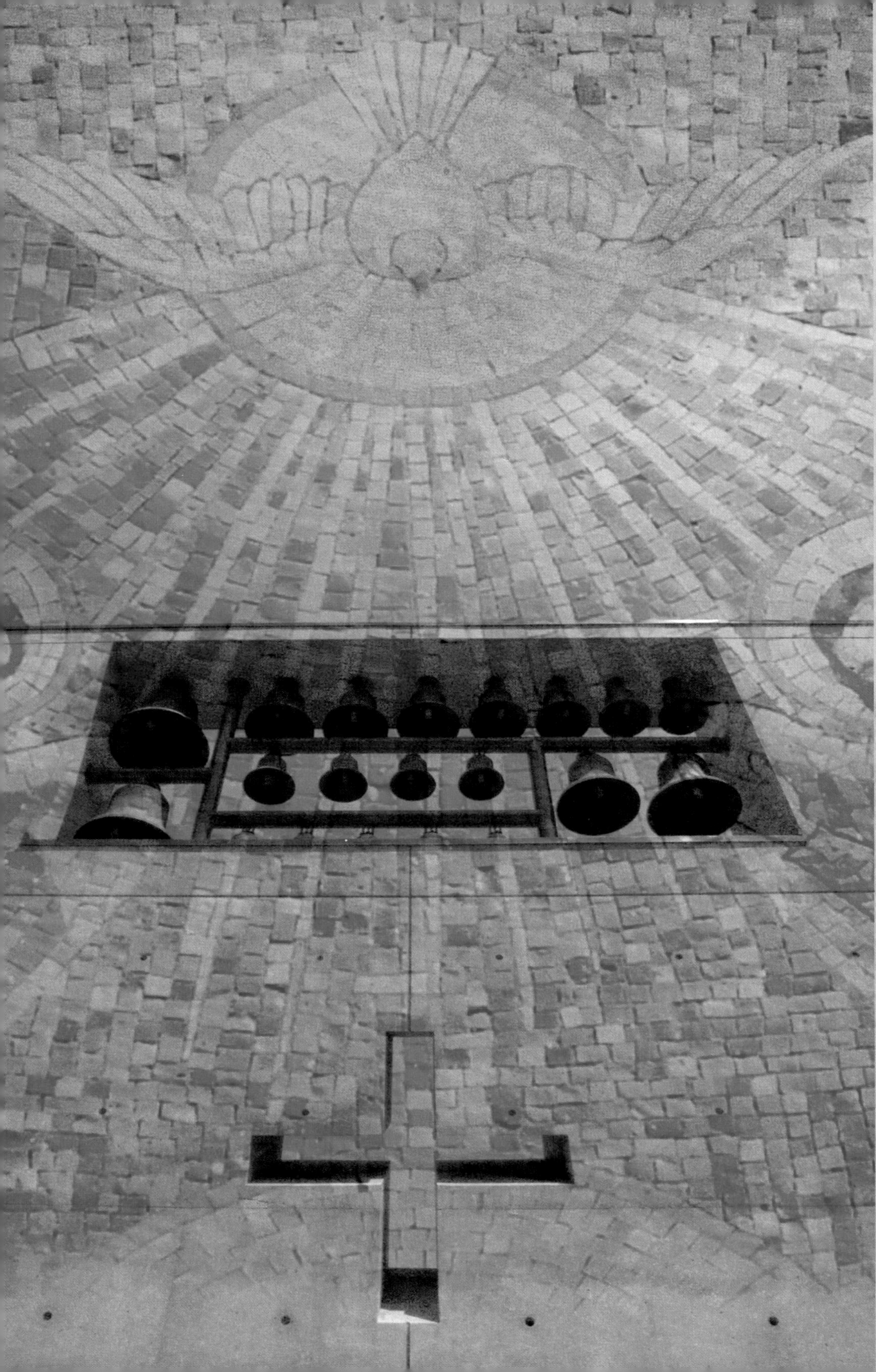

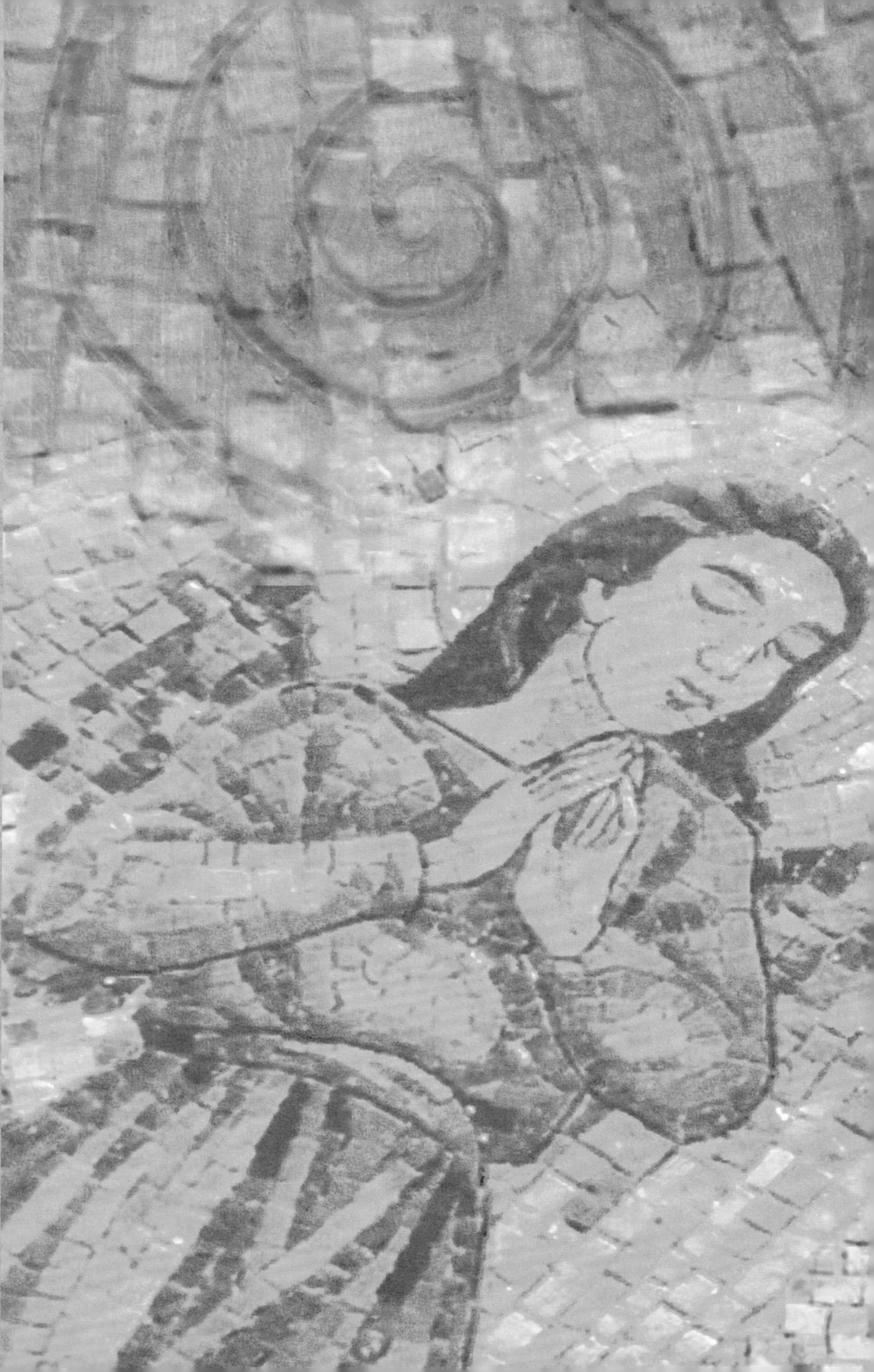

"I have hidden thy word in my heart."
—*Psalm 119:11*

At the same time, a pair of books included in our Bibles today barely made it in. One was 2 Peter. The early Church almost rejected that book, due to questions regarding its authorship. Bible scholars today believe 2 Peter was written between 100 and 150 CE, too late to have been authored by the Apostle Peter. Early Christians were also suspicious that someone had written the book falsely claiming the apostle's name.

The most emotional debates concerned the book of Revelation. Almost as soon as it was written (90–100 CE), the book had both fans and opponents. It is unlike any other New Testament book. Since the book contains many strange symbolic images, end-time fanatics have repeatedly misused Revelation. At the same time, Revelation has comforted many Christians suffering persecution. Debates over Revelation's place in the canon continued for nine hundred years, until it finally won out and was included.

METHODS USED TO SELECT THE BOOKS OF THE BIBLE

How did the leaders of the Christian churches choose which books should and which should not be included in the New Testament? Each book first passed several vital tests. One test was usage—or popularity. Books that were used for reading and worship in most of the churches were chosen, and those that were not commonly used were rejected.

Popularity was not the only test, however. A second test was more critical. In the first centuries of Christianity, a word-of-mouth record of Jesus's life and teachings existed alongside the written records. Early believers trusted these living memories of Jesus as much as the written accounts. If a Christian living around 100 CE had a question about Jesus,

he could go and talk with someone who had been friends with Apostle Peter or Apostle John. These living memories were the crucial factor in the acceptance or rejection of prospective Bible books. Christian leaders rejected writings that did not square with the spoken traditions regarding Jesus.

The leaders of the churches also asked if the writing inspired a holy life. Did the writing prove itself to be holy or inspired through the effects it produced in readers? Only books that passed these tests were included.

"These things are written so you may believe Jesus is the Christ, the Son of God, and believing you may have life in his name."

—*The Gospel of John 20:31*

WHY WERE THE GNOSTIC GOSPELS NOT INCLUDED?

Scores of books have been written about the "lost Gospels" found at Nag Hammadi in Egypt. Why did these Gnostic Gospels not make it into the New Testament?

First, the Gnostic Gospels appeared too late. The Gnostics wrote their Gospels more than a hundred years after the canonical Gospels and the letters of Paul. (The Gospel of Thomas is the one exception, discussed later.) Imagine if someone today wrote a book claiming to have new information concerning George Washington, information that contradicted previous historical records. Such a book would not be regarded in the same light as *primary sources* written by people who had actually known Washington.

In addition, the Gnostic Gospels failed when compared to the spoken traditions regarding Jesus. The Bishop Irenaeus asked, "If Jesus imparted secret knowledge to certain followers, why did he not do so with any of those who were leaders of the church?" The Gnostics composed their gospels claiming authorship by Peter, Thomas, and John. Yet people who had known these disciples denied any similarity between their teachings and those of the Gnostics.

The Gnostic Gospels offer little if any historical record of Jesus of Nazareth. However, they do offer a radically different vision of Christianity.

Chapter 3

RELIGION & MODERN CULTURE

THE GNOSTICS

Marcia and Dosia sat side by side under a shady tree, their hands deftly twirling strands of wool onto spindles. To a casual observer, the two friends were busy working, but in fact, the intellectual subjects they talked about were far more important to the two women than their physical handiwork. They were earnestly discussing two different forms of the Christian faith they shared.

"Have you heard the new preacher, Valentinus?" asked Dosia. "His teachings are so fascinating, and they stir such emotions within me—it is like drinking fine wine when I hear him."

Marcia furrowed her brow. "Yes, I have heard him, and his teachings intrigue me, also. Yet I heard Bishop Irenaeus when he spoke in Lyons last Sunday: the Bishop says that Valentinus is dangerous, that he will lead us away from the teachings of our Lord."

"I have not seen Bishop Irenaeus in a long time," replied Dosia, "and he seems a nice enough man. But I do not believe that Valentinus leads people away from Christ, rather he claims to know secret lessons that Christ entrusted to Mary Magdalene and others."

Marcia nodded. "I have heard him say the same, and I wonder who to believe. Bishop Irenaeus says the Church holds all the teachings of Christ in the four Gospels, and he says that Valentinus's secret teachings are nothing but lies."

Dosia became more excited. "Valentinus knows that some doubt his words, and he told us to pray to the Spirit of God within ourselves, and ask what is true. I have done that, and I believe that Sophia, Divine Wisdom herself, answered my prayers and said, 'Yes, these secret sayings are true.'"

Marcia put down her spindle and looked in her friend's eyes. "I am not sure who to believe, but I fear these two versions of our faith may divide people of faith from one another, and I earnestly hope they will not divide us, should we come to believe differently from each other."

THE BASICS OF GNOSTICISM

The word *gnosis* means "knowledge" in the Greek language. The Gnostics claimed to possess special knowledge of God and Christ, knowledge not possessed by other Christians. The *Eerdmans Dictionary of the Bible* defines Gnosticism as "a varied assortment of . . . religious movements."

It is uncertain when and how the Gnostic movement started, but Irenaeus first used the word Gnostic around the year 175 CE to describe

GLOSSARY

heretics: Those who hold beliefs that contradict established religious tradition, especially a belief that is condemned by religious authority.

pagan: Someone who does not follow one of the world's main religions, especially someone who is not a Christian, Muslim, or Jew, and whose religion is considered suspect.

paradoxical: Having the characteristic of being contradictory to itself.

people he said were *heretics*. Most experts agree, however, that the movement began before then. Some authors claim that *pagan* or Jewish Gnostics were around before Christianity became popular. Others see Gnosticism as a combination of early Christianity and Greek philosophy. Some of Paul's letters in the New Testament appear to be refutations of an early form of Gnosticism. No one knows how many people in early Christianity followed Gnostic teachings. Some respected historians believe there were more Gnostics than other kinds of Christians by the third century. They lost influence, however, in the following years.

For centuries, scholars knew about the Gnostics only from what they could glean from letters written denouncing the Gnostics. Irenaeus and other leaders of the early Christian church had little good to say about them. At the beginning of the twentieth century, however, portions of Gnostic writings surfaced in Egypt. In 1945, researchers hit the jackpot of Gnostic studies when a large clay jar containing a complete library was unearthed at Nag Hammadi, Egypt. Scholars quickly translated these documents.

These glimpses into a form of Christianity very different from that in the Bible fascinated religious freethinkers. Recently, a variety of authors have popularized Gnosticism. Dan Brown's novel *The Da Vinci Code* has caused a storm of controversy claiming the Gnostic Gospel of Philip proves Jesus had a sexual relationship with Mary Magdalene. New-Age author Margaret Starbird paints a compelling image of the Gnostics as the "faithful Charismatics of this hidden church" who trusted "the guidance of the Holy Spirit in every aspect of life" and revered Mary Magdalene, "the Goddess in the Gospels." On a much more scholarly level, Elaine Pagels has written a number of books in which she documents Gnosticism as part of the greatly varied Christian movement in its first centuries. Also on a scholarly level, the Jesus Seminar has attempted to establish the Gnostic Gospel of Thomas as "the fifth Gospel" on a par historically with the four Gospels found in the New Testament.

Despite this abundance of writing, describing the Gnostics is not an easy task. The Gnostic writings are full of "hidden" meanings put in symbolic and *paradoxical* terms. No one knows for sure the meanings of these writings. In the twenty-first century, writers have often interpreted the Gnostics according to their own spiritual beliefs and wishes.

GNOSTIC BELIEFS

The term Gnostics describes a religious grab bag. Some so-called Gnostics were similar to other Christians. Others held a very different set of beliefs. The beliefs of the Gnostics varied widely.

The Gnostics had a complex set of myths regarding God, angels,

ϲΟΦΊΑ

YOU SAY GNOSTIC—
WE SAY SOMETHING ELSE

Irenaeus used the term *Gnostic* to describe this group with very different beliefs from his own. A religious scholar in 1669 made use of the word, and ever since it has been used to describe this movement in early Christianity. However, in all the Gnostic texts—and there are many of them—they never use that word to describe themselves. They called themselves "offspring of Seth; chosen people; enlightened ones, the immovable race, and the perfect."

and the universe. According to Gnostic thinking, above all other beings was a God of pure Spirit, called Father-Mother or Father of All. From this God of pure Spirit flowed a series of lesser beings. Between the Father-Mother and the world of humans were scores of supernatural beings called powers, principalities, archons, and so on. Gnostic religious writings describe these in detail.

From the Father-Mother came forth the two most powerful manifestations of God, a male and female element. The male element was the Son of God, Christ, or Immortal Man. The female element was Sophia, or Wisdom. Together, Christ and Sophia brought forth the hosts of

THE GNOSTICS

43

good spiritual powers. Unfortunately, Sophia became proud and decided to produce a spirit from her own being, apart from partnership with Christ. This was a perversion of the perfect spiritual pattern, so this new being was evil.

The flawed child of Sophia is Yaldabaoth, also known as Yahweh. He is the god of the Old Testament. Yaldabaoth created the earth. Since Yaldabaoth was himself an illegitimate deity, the world he created was sinful and distorted. According to this line of thought, planet earth is a cosmic mistake! Yaldabaoth then created Adam, depraved like his creator.

Gnostic beliefs regarding creation are the opposite of those in the Bible. In Judaism and biblical Christianity, human beings are the good creation of a good God. The earth and human bodies are positive, not evil substances.

In one version of the Gnostic creation myth, Sophia, alarmed at what she had done, tried to straighten things out by sending Eve. Sophia created the first woman from a drop of her own essence. Yaldabaoth attempted to imprison Adam in the Garden of Eden by forbidding him to eat from the tree of knowledge (Gnosis). Eve freed Adam by granting him access to this forbidden knowledge. Again, this version of the creation myth is opposite that in the Hebrew Bible.

In Gnosticism, Christ comes to earth in order to free mortals from the limitations of their physical state. The Gnostics differed among themselves regarding Christ's nature. In some of their writings, he is the God-man who died on the cross and rose again, similar to other Christians' beliefs. However, in other Gnostic writings, Christ only appeared human; he was divine but lacked a human body. He only *appeared* to die on the cross; it was an illusion.

According to Gnostic beliefs, salvation came by connection with the mystical Christ inside of oneself. Only certain people, those born with special sensitivity, were able to achieve salvation. The secret teachings of Christ, contained in the Gnostic writings, helped people reach

45

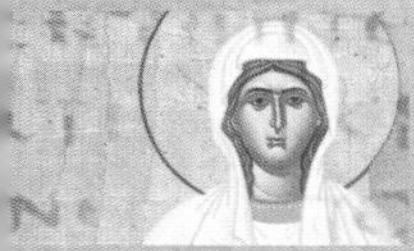

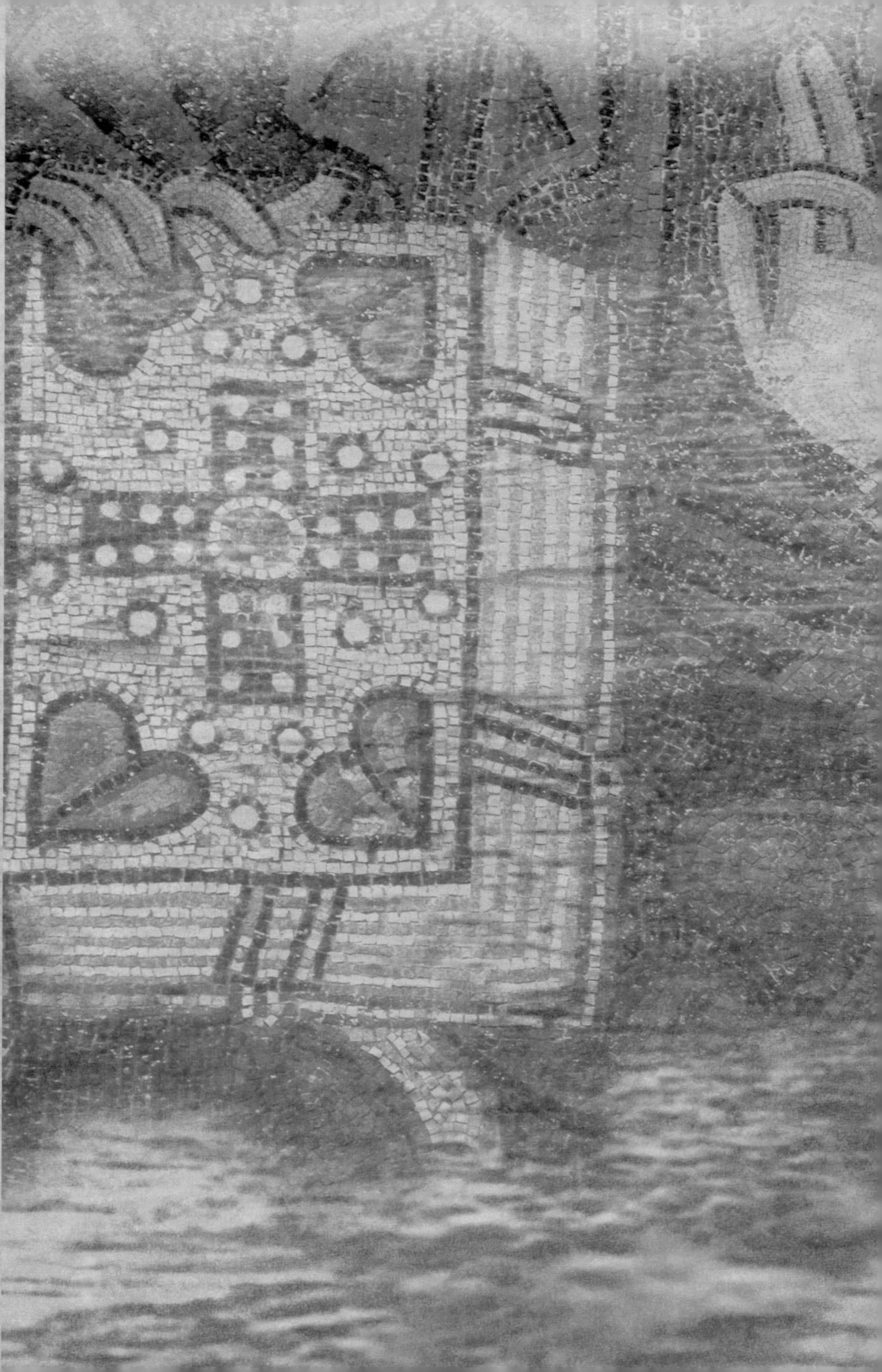

"Jesus said, 'Let one who seeks not stop seeking until he finds. When he finds, he will be troubled. When he is troubled, he will be astonished and rule over all."

—*from the second verse of* The Gnostic Gospel of Thomas

spiritual insight and freedom from the downward pull of their physical bodies. After learning the secrets of Gnosis and receiving baptism again, one becomes "perfect" and "spiritual."

Gnostic writings differ regarding the afterlife. Some texts suggest that all persons will eventually come to achieve freedom from the material world. In other letters, those who refuse Gnostic religion suffer in eternal flames.

The Gnostics believed Spirit and matter were always opposed to one another. Spirit was good, while anything material tended to be sinful. Since they despised the human body, Gnostics were apt to also despise marriage, sex, and childbirth. Their religion was ascetic; that is, they believed Christians must deny physical pleasure of all sorts to become spiritual. Some of the Gnostics' opponents claimed that the Gnostics engaged in religious sex rituals; Dan Brown refers to this idea in *The Da Vinci Code.* However, the Gnostics' own writings suggest the opposite.

GNOSTIC FEMINISTS?

Modern scholars have been particularly interested in Gnostic attitudes toward women. Some have suggested that Gnosticism was more accepting of women's rights than was the ancient Catholic Church. Other scholars question such views. They point out that Christian leaders of

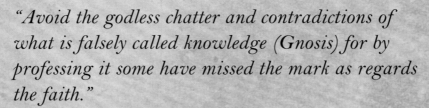

"Avoid the godless chatter and contradictions of what is falsely called knowledge (Gnosis) for by professing it some have missed the mark as regards the faith."

—*1 Timothy 6; Bible scholars say this may possibly refer to the beginnings of the Gnostic movement.*

the Middle Ages did indeed look down on women, but Christianity did not start out that way.

The Gnostics placed more emphasis on the Divine Feminine than did other early Christians. Before the creation of the world, Sophia is Christ's partner, an equal part of the deity. The Gnostics allowed women to teach in the churches and regarded Mary Magdalene as one of the key leaders among the disciples.

Nevertheless, the Gnostics were not entirely affirming of women. Sophia is part of the divine power, yet it is her poor choice that brings the evil of physical nature into the universe. The Letter of Peter to Philip says, "We are the ones who have suffered through the transgressions of the Mother."

The Gnostics, with their negative view of the body, looked down on childbirth. The most famous Gnostic Gospel, the Gospel of Thomas, ends with these words:

Simon Peter said, "Let Mary leave us, for women are not worthy of life." Jesus said, "I myself shall lead her, in order to make her male, so that she too may become a living spirit resembling you males. For every woman who makes herself male will enter the Kingdom of heaven."

Contrasting with this, Paul's letter to the Galatians, in the New Testament, affirmed, "There is neither male nor female . . . you are all one in Christ Jesus." Historian Thomas Cahill states, "Women were as

free to speak, to evangelize, and to administer the Pauline churches as was any man." Ben Witherington III, one of the most noted New Testament scholars, says, "I want to assure women that the New Testament documents are far more affirming of women and their roles in the church and society than most of the Gnostic documents."

WAS MARY MAGDALENE JESUS'S WIFE?

A key concept in *The Da Vinci Code* is that Jesus and Mary Magdalene were sexual companions. Quoting the Gnostic Gospel of Philip, the fictional character Leigh Teabing reads, "And the companion of the Savior is Mary Magdalene. Christ loved her more than all the disciples and used to kiss her often on the mouth." Teabing goes on to explain, "As

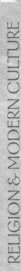

MARY·HATH·CHOSEN·THAT·GOOD·PART·WHICH
SHALL·NOT·BE·TAKEN·AWAY·FROM·HER

any Aramaic scholar will tell you, the word *companion* in those days literally meant *spouse.*"

Teabing says the language of the Gospel of Philip is Aramaic. However, the Gnostic gospels are all written in Coptic. In Coptic texts, the word "companion" is an expression of spiritual kinship, not marriage. Teabing also suggests the Gospel of Philip is more ancient than the Gospels in the Bible. In fact, scholars agree that someone wrote the Gospel of Philip centuries after the New Testament Gospels, and it contains no information regarding the historical Jesus. Jesus kisses James on the mouth in another Nag Hammadi text. Does that make Jesus gay? No. In Gnostic literature, a kiss from Jesus is a sign of spiritual enlightenment.

The ancient Catholic Church taught that Jesus had a physical body. They affirmed that married sex was good. In response to *The Da Vinci Code,* a number of Christian representatives have said, "It would have been fine if Jesus had married—he would still be both God and man." On the other hand, many of the ancient Gnostics denied that Jesus had a physical body. Furthermore, they looked down on sex, marriage, and anything related to physical bodies. The historical "facts" in *The Da Vinci Code* are backward. The Gnostics would be less likely than other Christians would be to accept the idea of a married Savior.

We can gain a more detailed understanding of Gnostic faith by looking at the sacred writings they left behind. We are able to read their version of scripture because of a spectacular find in Egypt, in 1945. The Nag Hammadi Library—the Lost Gospels—are a source of controversy and fascination for the twenty-first century.

RELIGION & MODERN CULTURE

LOST GOSPELS

Muhammad Ali al-Samman was committed to a dire deed. Along with his brothers,
he was on the trail of his father's murderer—and they would not rest until the
killer lay bleeding to death on the hot
Egyptian sand. Before that happened, however, the brothers would accidentally make
one of the greatest archaeological discoveries of the twentieth century.

"Jesus says: 'Love thy brother like thy soul; watch over him like the apple of thine eye.'"

—*Gospel of Thomas, verse 25*

Stopping to dig for fertilizer near the village of Nag Hammadi, the brothers chanced upon an enormous clay jar. It looked as if someone had buried it a long time ago. They debated what to do. Should they break it open? It might contain an evil spirit—or *jinn*—perhaps they had better not. Then, too, it might contain a treasure! They broke open the top and pulled out leather-bound books containing sheets of papyrus. They saw no value in these old pieces of paper, so they sent them home to serve as fuel for the family's oven.

A few weeks later, the brothers happened upon their father's murderer. They cut off his limbs, tore out his heart, and ate it. Egyptian police arrested al-Samman and investigated the brutal killing. While al-Samman was in jail, investigators looked through his home—and a local history teacher, Raghib, happened to see the ancient books and realized they were of value. The writings passed, in turn, from the teacher to a priest to a black-market dealer to the Egyptian government. Today the world knows these books as the Nag Hammadi Library.

Some modern religious seekers have chosen the Gnostic writings in the Nag Hammadi Library as their own scriptures. Elaine Pagels talks about how the Nag Hammadi writings allow a more diverse approach to Christianity. She likes the way the Gospel of Thomas and other writings encourage Christians to find truth inside themselves.

People of faith who are interested in a variety of religions also find the Gnostic writings appealing. The Gospel of Philip and other Gnostic documents are more like Zen Buddhism than are the New Testament Gospels. **New-Agers**, who tend to combine diverse religious beliefs, also appreciate the Eastern perspective of Gnostic texts. Even pagans and

GLOSSARY

New-Agers: People who believe in the cultural movement emphasizing spiritual consciousness, often involving belief in reincarnation and astrology and the practice of meditation and vegetarianism.

Zoroastrian: Following the beliefs of Zoroastrianism, including the principal beliefs that there is a supreme being and there is a cosmic contest between good and evil spirits.

Wiccans, who worship the Goddess, voice agreement with Gnostic verses that speak of Sophia and the Mother-Father.

CONTENTS OF THE NAG HAMMADI LIBRARY

The large clay jar found near Nag Hammadi, Egypt, in 1945 contained twelve books bound with leather covers. Ancient scribes had dried and pressed leaves of papyrus plants to form the pages. The books were all written in Coptic, an ancient Egyptian language. These twelve books contained forty-five separate titles.

Unknown persons buried them shortly before 400 CE. In 367, Bishop Athanasius wrote a letter from Alexandria, Egypt, condemning sacred writings outside of the Bible. It is likely someone hid these books at that time.

Modern writers often refer to the Nag Hammadi texts as "lost Gospels" or "lost books of the Bible." It is certainly true they were lost. For more than 1,500 years, no one could read these books. However, leaders of the ancient Christian churches did not regard them as books of the Bible. They are not "lost" Bible books in the sense of having been removed from the canon of scripture.

Although commonly referred to as a "Gnostic library," the Nag Hammadi books are not limited to one religious view. Some are indeed Gnostic. Others contain Greek philosophy, as well as Jewish and **Zoroastrian** religious ideas. They vary greatly.

THE GOSPEL OF THOMAS

In recent years, two books have popularized the Gospel of Thomas. The Jesus Seminar included Thomas in its work *The Five Gospels.* Professor Elaine Pagels wrote a popular book titled *Beyond Belief,* connecting her own spiritual discoveries at a time of grief with insights from the Gospel of Thomas.

The Gospel of Thomas is the earliest of the Nag Hammadi texts. In fact, Bible professor Stevan Davies thinks that it existed before any of the four canonical Gospels. Elaine Pagels is convinced that John wrote his Gospel as a response to the Gospel of Thomas. On the other hand, Ben Witherington III of Asbury Seminary says the opposite. He believes Thomas wrote to counter John. Scholars mostly agree that someone wrote the Gospel of Thomas around 100 CE, after John's Gospel was finished.

A GUIDE TO THE ROUGH LIFE

The Nag Hammadi Library texts do share one common idea. According to Professor Ben Witherington III, they all promote an ascetic life. At the time when someone buried the texts, Christians who wanted to live lives of extreme spiritual commitment had fled from the cities of Egypt. They thought the cities and villages were filled with all kinds of sin. These so-called Desert Fathers lived as hermits. Some lived in tiny caves. A few sat on stone pillars for years at a time. They lived on very little food. Women they avoided like the plague. The Nag Hammadi texts may have been important to these desert hermits because they encouraged their extreme lifestyle.

Unlike the other Gnostic books, Thomas may contain actual sayings of Jesus—but not many of them. The Jesus Seminar says only two sayings unique to the Gospel of Thomas are likely the words of Jesus. One of these is verse 97:

Jesus says: "The Kingdom of the Father is like a woman who takes a vessel of flour and sets out on a long road. The handle of the vessel broke: the flour spilled out on the road behind her without her knowing it and stopping it. When she arrived at the house she put the vessel down and found it was empty."

Christan Amundsen is a psychotherapist and minister of a modern Gnostic church. Amundsen explains this parable: "Like people who are unaware that they are leaking the stuff of their being, they walk along a road mindless until they find themselves empty. . . . Our lives, Jesus is saying, are lived by accident. We become 'broken jars,' with nothing inside."

The other verse the Jesus Seminar considers a likely original saying of Christ is verse 98:

> The Kingdom of the Father is like a man who wants to kill an important person. In his house, he unsheathed the sword and stuck it in the wall to assure himself that his hand would be firm. Then he killed the person.

New Testament expert F. F. Bruce writes, "This parable . . . may have come from a period when Zealot activity gave it contemporary relevance." (The Zealots were religious guerrillas who assassinated Roman occupiers in the Holy Land.) The verse may speak of the degree of commitment and forethought that the Kingdom of God requires from its followers.

Another Bible scholar, Bruce Chilton, considers verse 82 to be an authentic Jesus saying from the Gospel of Thomas: "Jesus says: 'He who is near me is near the fire, and he who is far from me is far from the

Kingdom.'" Funk and Hoover, of the Jesus Seminar, note, "To approach the divine is to risk danger."

THE APOCRYPHON OF JOHN

Gnostics loved complicated mythologies. The Apocryphon of John, composed around 185 CE, is an important summary of Gnostic myths. It is hard to imagine how anyone could memorize the "secrets" of the Gnostic religion, considering the huge amount of detail in the Apocryphon of John and similar writings. The creation of Adam takes two entire chapters. These chapters also list the angelic "authorities" Yaltabaoth used while making humans. The story begins, "Eteraphaope-Abron created his head; Meniggesstroeth created the brain; Asterechme created the right eye; Thaspomocha created the left eye," and on it goes for several more pages.

Frederica Mathewes-Green is a noted writer and religious commentator. Mathewes-Green believes Gnosticism ended because it was "just too complicated." Regarding complex mythologies like the Apocryphon of John, she says, "Your salvation depended on getting it right." That must have been daunting! Mathewes-Green says that in the end, "Gnosticism died under its own weight."

THE GOSPEL OF PHILIP

This Gospel, written by an anonymous Gnostic around 300 CE, contains few sayings or stories of Jesus. It appears to be a catechism, a religious instruction book.

The Gospel of Philip is full of mysterious sayings. Some readers have likened these to koans in the Zen Buddhist tradition. Koans do not

> *"His disciples said: Teach us about the place where you are, for it is necessary for us to seek it. He said to them: He who has ears, let him hear! There is light within a man of light, and he lights the whole world. If he does not shine, there is darkness."*
>
> —*Gospel of Thomas, verse 24*

have an obvious meaning; instead, they challenge the reader to think. As the Gospel of Philip says, "Names given to the world are very deceptive." According to the Gnostic author of Philip, one must go beyond words to attain spiritual truth. A typical passage says:

> A **gentile** does not die, for he has never lived in order that he may die. He who has believed in the truth has found life, and this one is in danger of dying, for he is alive. Since Christ came the world has been created, the cities adorned, the dead carried out. When we were Hebrews we were orphans and had only our mother, but when we became Christians we had both father and mother.

Some modern readers find such sayings frustrating and confusing. Other readers delight in figuring out the hidden meanings of such sayings. The modern reaction to the books of the Nag Hammadi Library helps us understand why many early Christians became Gnostics—and why many others remained with the clearer teachings of the New Testament.

Modern fascination with alternative religion does not end with the Gnostics. Secretive religious groups, such as the Knights Templar and the Priory of Sion, also provide alternative ways to understand religion. These groups are part of a completely different way to view the world—one that involves conspiracy theories.

Chapter 5

CONSPIRACIES & SECRET SOCIETIES

RELIGION & MODERN CULTURE

In 1947, a flying saucer crashed near Roswell, New Mexico. Government agents rushed in to take away the saucer and the bodies of its extraterrestrial pilots. The government keeps the alien bodies and technology from the crash hidden inside a top-secret government complex called Area 51. They are using information from the saucer crash to create new technology. This alien technology has enabled us to make rapid advances in computers, space flight, and other high-tech fields. The government also uses alien technology to protect citizens from the extraterrestrials, who still visit our planet on a regular basis.

Since the eighteenth century, all national governments have only been puppets. Politicians actually hold little real power. A secret organization called the Illuminati really rules the world. They have agents in all the top military and financial posts of governments around the globe. Their eventual aim is a one-world government. The European Union, centralized computer systems, and other recent changes in the world are all part of their plan.

For 2,000 years, the Catholic Church has hidden the truth about Jesus Christ. The Bible was invented by the Church to create the myth that Jesus was divine. In fact, he was an ordinary man who married an extraordinary woman—Mary Magdalene. Secret religious societies have protected their children and their descendants for countless generations since then. The Cathars, Knights Templar, and the Priory of Sion guarded the secret bloodline of Jesus. The famous artist Leonardo da Vinci left clues to this secret in his paintings. The Catholic Church has done all it could—burned heretics, paid bribes, even murdered—to keep this information hidden.

What do these three scenarios have in common? All three are conspiracy theories. Conspiracy theories claim that a secret organization is hiding an enormous secret from the rest of the world. The fact that most people disagree with them just shows how secret the conspiracy is. A recent *Newsweek* article said, "At the end of an exhausting century, conspiracy is a comfortable way to make sense of a messy world. . . . Things don't just fall apart. Somebody makes them fall apart."

In *The Da Vinci Code*, Dan Brown draws from an assortment of popular conspiracy theories to make plausible what his character Leigh Teabing calls "the greatest cover-up in human history." The notion of the Jesus-Magdalene bloodline is hardly new. Dan Brown got the majority of his ideas for *The Da Vinci Code* from a book called *Holy Blood, Holy Grail*, published in 1982 and written by Michael Baigent, Richard Leigh,

GLOSSARY

gentile: Someone who is not Jewish.

anti-Semitic: Hating or discriminating against Jewish people.

nationalist: Supporting strong devotion to one nation and its interests above all others.

and Henry Lincoln. *The Da Vinci Code* followed the ideas of their work so closely that Baigent and Leigh sued Brown for plagiarizing their book.

As we take a look at the groups mentioned in *The Da Vinci Code* and *Holy Blood, Holy Grail* as protectors of the great secret, it is important to separate fact from fiction. Be aware, however, that in the history of secret organizations and suppressed religions, fact and fantasy sometimes lie close together.

THE CATHARS

The Cathars play no role in *The Da Vinci Code* but are significant in *Holy Blood, Holy Grail*. According to Baigent and his coauthors, the Catholic Church destroyed the Cathars because of their belief that Jesus and Magdalene were married.

RELIGION & MODERN CULTURE

"The truth is out there."

—*Fox Mulder, from* The X-Files

The name "Cathar" comes from the Greek word meaning "pure" or "purified." Cathar beliefs were similar to those of the Gnostics. Those who fully accepted Cathar beliefs underwent a second baptism. After that, they lived rigorous ascetic lives. They called themselves *perfecti*—spiritually perfect ones.

Perfecti men avoided women. No perfecti could touch a pregnant woman since they connected pregnancy with the sinfulness of sexual intercourse. According to the Cathars, marriage was a form of prostitution. Given such beliefs, it is not surprising there are no Cathar records alleging marriage between Christ and Magdalene.

In 1209, Pope Innocent III declared a Crusade against the Cathars. Thirty-four years later, ten thousand Catholic soldiers surrounded the Cathar remnant in the fortress called Montsegur. By March of 1244, after a ten-month siege, it was clear the castle would fall. Four men slipped over the walls and disappeared, taking with them something called "the Cathar treasure." A few days later, the population of the fortress surrendered, and the Catholic troops burned all the Cathars at the stake. Right up to their death, none of the Cathars told what the escaped "treasure" was. In the centuries since then, many people have speculated. Some believe the treasure was the Holy Grail. Others suggest it may have been Gnostic writings. Or, perhaps it was literal treasure—silver and gold donated to the Cathar church. The secret of the Montsegur treasure disappeared into history, along with the end of the Cathar religion.

51

THE KNIGHTS TEMPLAR

According to Leigh Teabing in *The Da Vinci Code*, during the Middle Ages the Knights Templar discovered a treasure underneath the site of Solomon's Temple in Jerusalem. This treasure was the Sangreal Documents, which told the story of Christ's union with Magdalene. The Knights Templar used the Sangreal Documents to hold power over the Catholic Church, until the Church wiped them out in order to suppress these potentially scandalous materials.

The Sangreal Documents are pure fiction, but the Knights Templar were a fascinating part of medieval history. After the First Crusade captured Jerusalem, a small band of knights took sacred vows to protect Christian pilgrims traveling in the Holy Land. They originally survived on donations and called themselves the Poor Knights of Christ.

At the time, Bernard of Clairvaux, founder of the Cistercian order of monks, was a popular writer and speaker. Bernard supported the Knights, and the Church gave this military order headquarters on top of the site of Solomon's Temple in Jerusalem. Thereafter, people called them "Templars."

The Templars were warrior monks, sworn to serve Christ as knights in armor. They lived by the strict standards of religious orders—living with few comforts, chanting prayers throughout the day, and listening to readings from the Bible while they ate. They avoided the company of women, believing it led to sexual temptation. They were bold fighters who built large castles and controlled the Holy Land for a century. The Templars governed the Middle Eastern trade routes and became influential in the business world. The pope allowed them to raise taxes in the areas they controlled. Before long, they were no longer "the poor knights of Christ." In fact, they were wealthy.

Muslim armies drove the Templars out of the Holy Land in 1291. They continued for another sixteen years in Europe, but with the loss

of the Holy Land, they lost their sacred mission. The king of France, Philip the IV, resented their wealth. On Friday, October 13, 1307, by command of King Philip, all Templars in France were seized, and their property was confiscated. The knights were tortured to extract confessions, and the Templar leaders were burned at the stake. Their Grand Master, Jacques de Molay, died shouting that he was a faithful Christian. He called the pope and king who accused him to meet at the Judgment Seat of Christ. Within a year, both the pope and king died unexpectedly, creating public sympathy for the martyred Templar.

While being tortured, Templars confessed to worshipping something they called *Baphomet*. There have been a number of guesses as to the actual nature of the Templar idol Baphomet. It may have been the French word at the time for Mohammed, hence a confession of Templars having "given in to the enemy."

British biblical scholar Hugh Schonfield has suggested that Baphomet is in a form of code called the Atbash Cipher. In *The Da Vinci Code*, Dan Brown alludes to this with a clue that says, "Atbash will reveal the truth to thee." Using numbers for Hebrew letters, Schonfield

discovered that "Baphomet" reads "Sophia." Dan Brown explains this in chapter 76 of his book. Did the Templars worship the feminine aspect of God called Sophia? There is no other evidence they did so. Like their supporter Bernard of Clairvaux, the Templars were devoted to the Virgin Mary.

British historian Ian Wilson has suggested that the "bearded head" allegedly worshipped by the Templars may have been the Shroud of Turin. At that time, the Shroud may have been folded, revealing only the striking portrait of a bearded head covered with blood from a crown of thorns. (Read *The Grail, the Shroud, and Other Religious Relics: Secrets and Ancient Mysteries* in this series of books for more information on this topic.)

Medieval historians say the most likely solution to the meaning of Baphomet is—it never existed. Under torture, even strong men will confess to all sorts of things, and the tortures applied to the Templars were unspeakable. Confessions made under such conditions are hardly believable.

THE PRIORY OF SION

The Da Vinci Code begins with these words:

> FACT: The Priory of Sion—a European secret society founded in 1099—is a real organization. In 1975 Paris's Bibliothèque Nationale discovered parchments known as *Les Dossiers Secrets*, identifying numerous members of the Priory of Sion, including Sir Isaac Newton, Botticelli, Victor Hugo and Leonardo Da Vinci.

As Simon Cox, editor of *Phenomena* magazine, points out, the invisible existence of the Priory of Sion "underpins the entire plot of *The Da Vinci Code*." The plot of *The Da Vinci Code* follows that of the book *Holy Blood, Holy Grail*, and the authors of *Holy Blood, Holy Grail* base their book

THE TRUTH IS OUT THERE

Through the 1990s, the weekly television show *The X-Files* covered every conspiracy theory imaginable. The producers presented the show as pure fantasy, but it drew legions of fans who agreed with FBI agent Fox Mulder's motto, "I want to believe." In one episode, a forger produced a phony Gospel of Mary Magdalene, which told of a sexual relationship between Mary and Jesus. A cardinal of the Catholic Church murdered the forger. Does this plot sound a bit familiar?

largely on the Dossiers Secrets of the Priory of Sion parchments. Thus, the Priory of Sion is the true key to *The Da Vinci Code*. If the documents of the Priory are real, then Dan Brown's book may indeed contain earth-shaking revelations regarding history and religion. If the Priory is a falsehood, then *The Da Vinci Code* is also fantasy.

Consider what a variety of researchers say about the Priory of Sion. Award-winning journalist Dan Burstein authored an article titled "The Hoax Behind It All" in *U.S. News & World Report Secrets of* The Da Vinci Code. Burstein writes, "Finally, the secret sect that first started it all off, the Priory of Sion, has been exposed as a fraud." Likewise, Laura Miller wrote a piece for the *New York Times* in 2004 titled *The Da Vinci Con*. She explains, "*The Da Vinci Code*, like *Holy Blood, Holy Grail*, is

based on a notorious hoax." Miller found "the legitimacy of the Priory of Sion history rests on . . . documents that even the authors of *Holy Blood, Holy Grail* suggest were planted in the Bibliothéque Nationale by a man named Pierre Plantard. As early as the 1970s, one of Plantard's confederates admitted to helping him fabricate the materials."

Furthermore, Amy Bernstein, a writer with a doctorate from Oxford in French literature, debunks the Priory of Sion myth. After researching the subject, she says, "My conclusion . . . is that beginning in the 1950s, a small group of men with . . . ***nationalist*** and sometimes ***anti-Semitic*** leanings was able to perpetrate what is almost certainly a . . . hoax that continues to draw people in today." She also traces the Priory of Sion hoax to Pierre Plantard. Bernstein notes, "He served four months in Fresnes prison in the early 1950s, convicted of fraud and embezzlement." She tells how a fellow forger, Gérard de Sède, published a book titled *Rennes—le Château: Le dossier, les impostures, les phantasmes, les hypotheses,* "in which he essentially admitted that the dossiers were forged." The story of the Priory of Sion is a fascinating work of fiction.

OPUS DEI

Throughout *The Da Vinci Code*, the albino giant Silas stalks Robert Langdon and Sophie Neveu. Silas works for Bishop Manual Aringarosa. Both Silas and the bishop are members of the Catholic organization Opus Dei.

According to Jesuit author James Martin, Opus Dei boasts 77,000 members worldwide, with more than 3,000 in the United States. Martin writes:

> To its members it is nothing less than the work of God, the inspiration of the blessed Josemaría Escrivá de Balaguer, who advanced the work of Christ by promoting sanctity in everyday life. To its critics it is a powerful, even dangerous, cult-like organization that uses secrecy and manipulation to advance its agenda.

Leaders of Opus Dei deny they are a "secret" organization. "But members have no reason to try to publicize their membership, because a lay person's approach to holiness in Opus Dei is something personal, an aspect of his or her private life."

As Dan Brown accurately states in *The Da Vinci Code*,

with the 1934 publication of Josemaría Escrivá's spiritual book *The Way*—*999 points of meditation for doing God's work in one's own life*—Escrivá's message exploded across the world. Now, with over four million copies of *The Way* in circulation in forty-two languages, Opus Dei was a global force.

"The truth is out there, but so are the lies."

—*Dana Scully, from* The X-Files

There are various classes of membership in Opus Dei. Only 2 percent of members are priests. Associate members live in their own homes and may be married and have children. Numeraries live in Opus Dei houses and are celibate; they give most of their income to the organization. In *The Da Vinci Code*, Silas is a numerary.

As explained by Stephen Tomkins in an article on the BBC Web site news.bbc.co.uk/2/hi/uk_news/magazine/4194567.stm,

> Opus Dei teaches that even the minutiae of life should be pleasing to God, from doing one's job well to being cheerful, from right beliefs to good manners. It puts a lot of emphasis on serving God through work. It encourages prayer, Bible-reading and Mass every day.

The most controversial practice of Opus Dei members is "corporal mortification," suffering physical discomfort in order to attain spiritual growth. In *The Da Vinci Code*, Silas wears a cilice belt, a spiked chain worn around the upper thigh for two hours a day by some numeraries. The cilice can leave small prick holes in the skin.

The official Opus Dei Web site says, "Some people in the history of the Church have felt called to undertake . . . sacrifices, such as frequent fasting or using a hair shirt, cilice, or discipline, as can be seen in the lives of many of those explicitly recognized by the Church as models of holiness." The Opus Dei site also claims, "Those who seek to advance in Christian perfection must mortify themselves more than ordinary believers are required to do."

51

> *"All the usual suspects . . . of paranoid history get caught up in this thousand-year jaunt. The Cathar heretics, the Knights Templar . . . the Vatican, the Freemasons, Nazis, the Dead Sea Scrolls—everyone but the Abominable Snowman seems to be in on the Game."*
>
> —Laura Miller, *commenting on* Holy Blood, Holy Grail
> *and* The Da Vinci Code

Few Christians—including Catholics—practice such painful exercises. Clearly, Opus Dei numeraries take their faith to its limits. At the same time, there is no record that any of them have assassinated someone, like Silas in *The Da Vinci Code.*

CONSPIRACIES & CODES

The Knights Templar, Priory of Sion, Opus Dei, and similar groups fascinate readers because of their alleged secret beliefs and practices. Constructing conspiracy theories is an intriguing game to play. Another game that's very similar is finding "hidden codes" in religious texts. *The Da Vinci Code* features the idea that Leonardo da Vinci hid secrets related to Jesus Christ in his artwork. In the novel, Dan Brown even suggests that Walt Disney cartoons convey hidden religious statements. At the same time, some religious conservatives claim that the Bible itself contains secret coded messages.

51

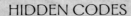

Chapter 6

HIDDEN CODES

Sophie Neveu, while speaking to Leigh Teabing in a climactic scene of *The Da Vinci Code*, realizes:

> The Holy Grail is a woman, Sophie thought, her mind a collage of interrelated ideas that seemed to make no sense. "You said you have a picture of this woman who you claim is the Holy Grail." Teabing . . . wheeled suddenly and pointed to the far wall. On it hung an eight-foot-long print of *The Last Supper*, the same exact image Sophie had just been looking at. "There she is!"

Dan Brown reveals the significance of the title for his suspense novel in chapters 55 through 58 of *The Da Vinci Code*. He suggests that the famous Renaissance artist Leonardo da Vinci was a member of the Priory of Sion. Furthermore, he says the artist left clues in his most famous painting, *The Last Supper*, pointing to Jesus's union with Mary Magdalene.

These claims fascinate readers. As the old saying goes, "Seeing is believing." Hidden messages are much more compelling if they are visual, revealed in a work of art. Millions of readers can literally see for themselves whether they agree with Brown's novel.

Again, Dan Brown claims he is expressing facts rather than fiction. In an interview on the *Today Show*, host Matt Lauer asked Dan Brown, "How much of this is based on reality in terms of things that actually occurred? I know you did a lot of research for the book." Dan Brown replied, "Absolutely all of it . . . all of the art, architecture, secret rituals, secret societies, all of that is historical fact."

A PHONY LEONARDO DA VINCI?

Before we look at Leonardo's art, let us take a moment to consider what the novel says about the artist himself, comparing the claims in this work of fiction with the historical record. In the novel, French police captain Bezu Fache says, "Leonardo Da Vinci had a tendency toward the darker arts." Robert Langdon adds to this, "he believed he possessed the alchemic power to turn lead into gold and even cheat God by creating an elixir to cheat death" (page 45). Fache associates Leonardo with evil magic, and Langdon associates the artist with alchemy, the medieval magic that led to the beginnings of modern chemistry. In actual history, Leonardo despised both magicians and alchemists.

In *The Da Vinci Code*, Leigh Teabing quotes Leonardo: "Many have made a trade of delusions and false miracles, deceiving the stupid multi-

SHOW & TELL

Dan Brown made some brilliant choices writing *The Da Vinci Code*. One was the emphasis on *symbols* and *art*. His wife, Blythe, to whom he dedicated the novel, is an art historian. Brown says she helps him look at artwork. This is especially fortunate because today's world is increasingly visual. Philosophers suggest that in the twenty-first century we have all moved from a print-based view of reality to an image-based view. If the past was "tell me," the present is "show me." *The Da Vinci Code* is a perfect suspense story for the twenty-first century because it shows as well as tells. This is especially true with the illustrated edition of the book, and will be even more so with the movie. Notice that the fictional character Robert Langdon is a symbologist. In a visual age, the hero is one who finds truth in images rather than words.

tudes." Sophie Neveu asks, "Da Vinci is talking about the Bible?" and Teabing nods. However, when historians read that quote in its original form, they find that Leonardo made those statements about alchemists. Dan Brown has changed the data so his novel presents the opposite of historical facts.

The novel also says Leonardo da Vinci "was anything but Christian" (page 45) and, "Leonardo was a well-documented devotee of the ancient ways of the goddess" (page 96). Historical records tell us that it is true Leonardo disagreed with some beliefs of the Catholic faith. He was more interested in science than religion. However, before his death he dictated his will to several witnesses. In his will, he entrusted his soul "to almighty God and the Virgin Mary." No records indicate he ever rejected God or worshipped any "goddess" besides the Virgin mother of Jesus.

> *"I know of no serious scholar who has proposed this notion."*
>
> *—Joseph Forte, art historian, responding to the idea that da Vinci's paintings depict a marriage between Jesus and Mary Magdalene*

A CLOSER LOOK AT "THE DA VINCI CODE"

The entire novel focuses on a painting, *The Last Supper*, and a series of statements regarding this work. These claims are as follows:

1. The figure to the right of Jesus is Mary Magdalene. She has "flowing red hair, delicate folded hands, and the hint of a bosom . . . without a doubt . . . female."
2. The figures of Jesus and Magdalene make a "V" shape, which is a symbol representing a female womb.
3. The figures of Jesus and Magdalene also form a perfect "M," which stands for Magdalene.
4. Peter is "leaning menacingly" toward Magdalene and "slicing his blade-like hand across her neck" as a symbolic portrayal of the tension between Peter and Magdalene described in a Gnostic Gospel.
5. The painting depicts a disembodied hand, three figures to the left of Jesus, holding a threatening dagger.
6. The Chalice, the cup of the last supper, is missing from the scene. According to the novel, it is missing because Magdalene herself is the chalice.

It seems odd yet is undeniably true that two people can stare at the same object and see completely different things. These are the things that Dan Brown sees when he looks at *The Last Supper*. Art experts see things differently.

First, is that a woman next to Jesus? Art experts agree the figure is the Apostle John, described as sitting next to Jesus in the Gospel of John. Furthermore, a sixteenth-century copy of *The Last Supper* actually labels each disciple, including John in that spot. Art historians agree the painting illustrates *The Last Supper* according to the Gospel of John, chapter 13.

The Apostle John does appear feminine in this painting. According to Diane Apostolos-Cappadona, professor of religious art at Georgetown University, "There is a tradition of John being seen in our eyes as soft, feminine, and youthful." There are other works of art, made around the same time or earlier, that show John as "a girly man." Consider the statue *St. John Resting on the Bosom of Christ* by Master Heinrich of Constance. The "Beloved Disciple" (a common term for John) in that statue looks very effeminate. In fact, he could easily pass for a girl. Elizabeth Lev, who teaches art history at Duquesne University's Rome campus, explains:

> John is portrayed, as is common in many Renaissance paintings, as the "student." A favored follower, a protégé or disciple, is always portrayed as very youthful, longhaired and clean-shaven; the idea being that he has not yet matured to the point where he must find his own way. Throughout the Renaissance, artists portray St. John in this fashion.

Now, what about the "V" shape formed between Christ and the figure to his right? The novel claims this "V" is the symbol for a womb, hence suggesting a woman. Art experts agree Leonardo deliberately formed the "V" at the center of the painting. The most likely reason? The "V" is good art composition. It draws the viewer's eye perfectly to the center of the picture. There is also a symbolic possibility. The letter

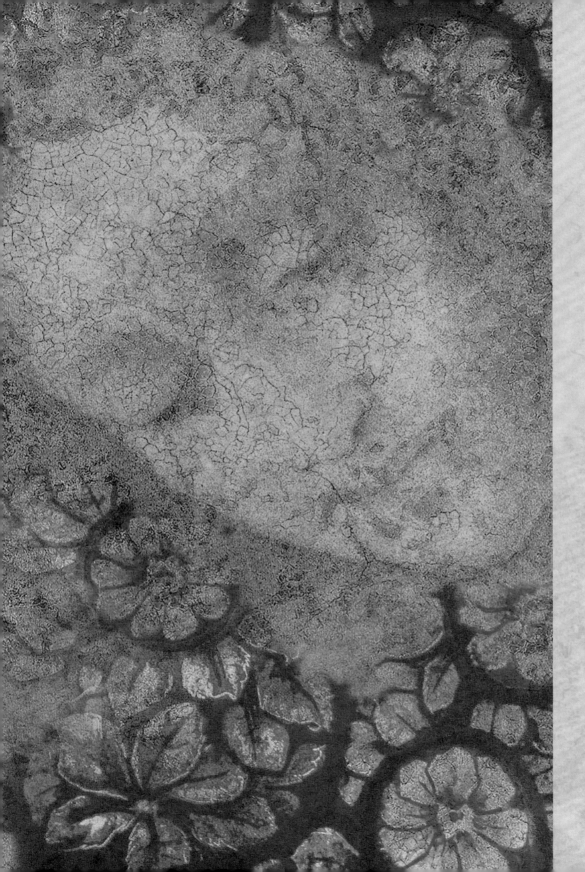

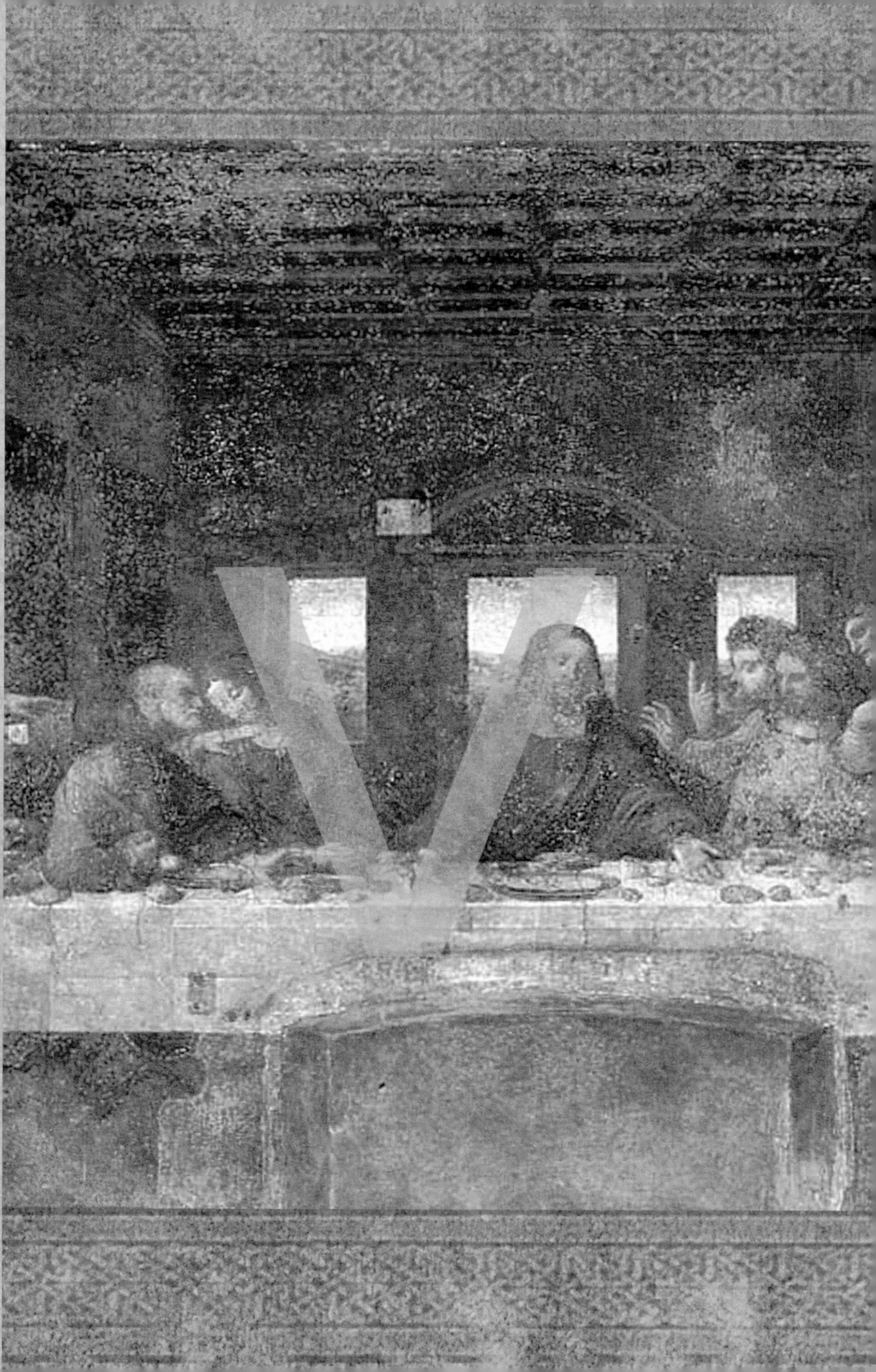
V

"V" could stand for *veritas*, the Latin word for truth. That would remind viewers of Jesus's words in John's Gospel, "I am the Truth."

What about the "M" formed by Jesus and the figure to his right? The novel claims it stands for "Magdalene." In response, art experts say, "What 'M'? We don't see any 'M.'" In fact, there are only three sides of an "M," forming something more like a bolt of lightning.

How about that menacing hand? According to Brown, Peter is giving the "cut your head off" message to the figure next to him. Art experts say the hand just happens to come across the neck of the Apostle John. In fact, the hand is pointing to Jesus. Rather than animosity, this pair of figures is consulting with one another. John is leaning his head back to talk with Peter.

What shall we make of the "disembodied" hand holding that rather large knife? In fact, the hand belongs to Peter. You can see that by looking at the picture, and an existing rough sketch by Leonardo proves the point. There is also a *reason* why Peter is holding that long knife. It is a religious symbol. According to the Gospel of John, Peter will soon draw his sword when the soldiers come for Jesus (John 18). Religious pictures from the Renaissance are full of such details.

Now for the biggest mystery according to *The Da Vinci Code*. "There was no chalice in the painting. No holy grail." Leigh Teabing tells Sophie Neveu, "'Oddly, Da Vinci appears to have forgotten the cup of Christ.'" Here, Dan Brown makes a blatantly false statement at one of the most critical points in the story. You can see for yourself. Get a high-resolution picture of *The Last Supper* taken after its restoration. Look on the table, to the inside of Jesus's left hand. An inch away from Christ's hand there is a glass cup, half filled with liquid. It is obviously Jesus's cup. Leonardo has not "forgotten the cup of Christ." Rather, he chose to paint it as an ordinary glass cup, rather than a big fancy goblet like the ones used in church.

Why did Leonardo paint the cup of Christ in this unspectacular way? His *Last Supper* is a portrayal of the scene described specifically in the

Gospel of John. In John's Gospel there is no mention of the cup of wine. Leonardo painted *The Last Supper* to highlight John's story of betrayal rather than the bread and wine on which the other Gospels focus. From this perspective, Leonardo was true to his subject.

There are indeed subtle religious details in Leonardo's painting. It is a brilliant piece of art that demands a second or third look.

THE DISNEY CODE

According to Dan Brown's fiction, Leonardo da Vinci was not the only great artist to hide religious secrets in his paintings. In chapter 61, "Robert Langdon held up his Mickey Mouse watch and told her that Walt Disney had made it his life's work to pass on the Grail story to future generations." Apparently, Walt Disney was also in on the 2,000-year-old Mary Magdalene secret. The novel goes on to say, "Like Leonardo, Walt Disney loved infusing hidden messages and symbolism in his art." The novel claims Disney filled his cartoons with "religion, pagan myth and stories of the subjugated goddess." Langdon explains that *Cinderella*, *Sleeping Beauty*, and *Snow White* portray the "sacred feminine." Snow White is a retelling of the Garden of Eden myth. *Sleeping Beauty* is the Grail myth for children. Furthermore, "The Little Mermaid was a spellbinding tapestry of symbols so specifically goddess related that they could not be coincidence."

Some readers might believe that the *Little Mermaid* is "a ninety-minute collage of blatant . . . references to . . . Isis, Eve, Pisces the fish goddess and, repeatedly, Mary Magdalene." Chapter 61 convinces other readers that Dan Brown can find religious symbols in everything and anything. Like conspiracy theories, the search for hidden religious codes is apparently limitless.

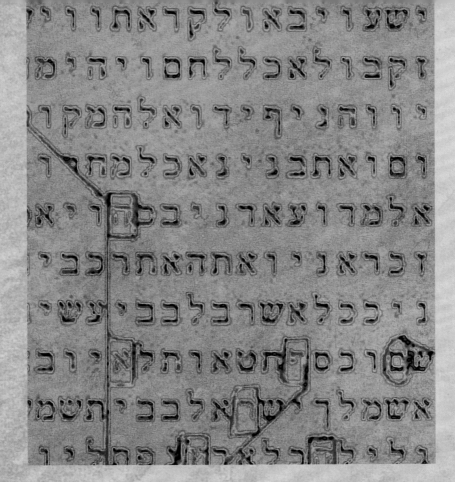

THE BIBLE CODE

What would you do if you discovered a coded message telling you an important world figure would soon be assassinated? In the early 1990s, Michael Drosnin, an investigative reporter who has written for the *Washington Post* and *Wall Street Journal,* heard that the Israeli mathematician Dr. Eliyahu Rips had discovered a secret code in the Bible. Supposedly, this code enabled Rips to predict the day the Gulf War would begin two months in advance. Drosnin says he was skeptical but went to check it out—and was convinced that Rips' discovery was

genuine. He also found a coded message that convinced him Yitzhak Rabin was in mortal danger. Drosnin says:

> I had found his murder encoded in the Bible more than a year before it happened and I flew to Israel to warn the prime minister. I gave a letter warning of this to a close friend who gave it to Rabin. . . . Then on Nov. 4th, 1995, I was at a train station talking to a friend on a pay phone. He told me Rabin had been murdered. I slid to the floor. The air went out of me. Up until then I thought the code was real intellectually, but then I knew in my heart.

The Bible code is what cryptologists (code scholars) call a "skip" code. The cryptologist arranges a large printed text—in this case the Hebrew Bible—into a large grid pattern. This looks like a crossword puzzle. Then the researcher runs a computer program that skips letters. For example, search every fifth letter. The program can search for words left, right, up, down, any direction. The searcher looks for words that have meaning when paired with other words. For example, Drosnin found the words Bill Clinton with president, and Kennedy with Dallas. Although Drosnin claims that computer decoding of the Hebrew Bible predicted Rabin's assassination, the Gulf War, and Bill Clinton's presidency, he also says, "I don't think the code makes predictions. I think it might tell us all our possible futures."

Curiously, when asked about his religion, Drosnin claims, "I am Jewish. But I am not at all religious, and don't believe in God." When asked who wrote the Bible code, Drosnin says, "I don't know. I'm a reporter and can't go past the hard evidence. There is a code, therefore there is an encoder. I don't know who or what it/he/she is."

Michael Drosnin is convinced, "The Bible code is an established fact." He claims that random chance could not create the results he has found. Furthermore, Drosnin says that other large texts fail to produce the same results.

Since the Bible code became popular, religious researchers have produced a multitude of similar results. Believers say the King James Version of the English Bible works the same way as the Hebrew Bible. Books and Internet sites report a steady stream of new Bible code discoveries. In February 2005, an Internet site claimed that words found in the Hebrew Bible predicted the tsunami that devastated India and

Indonesia. However, the discoverer did not post this information until *after* the horrible disaster. Also recently, a Bible decoder said he found a message in the King James Bible related to Michael Jackson. The crossword says, "Pop king false face painted he dies sad." Other decoded Bible messages include the attack on the World Trade Center and the UFO crash at Roswell.

Although Drosnin is certain the Bible code results are unique, skeptics are unimpressed. They claim similar results using the Hebrew language translation of *War and Peace*, and even using lengthy legal briefs. Christian and Jewish scholars scoff at the idea that either the Hebrew Bible or the King James Bible were composed precisely letter-by-letter by God. They know that over the centuries there have been numerous tiny changes in the text.

For some, the Bible code proves the Bible is a divine book. In addition, it can provide "insider" information about the future. Others say the Bible code simply proves that a computer can turn any big book into a giant crossword puzzle and then "find" words the programmer believes have meaning. Even Michael Drosnin admits, "You can only find what you know how to look for—you must have some idea of what you're looking for."

CHOOSING MY RELIGION & THE SCRIPTURES TO PROVE IT

For many North Americans in the past, the Holy Bible (usually the King James Translation) was Holy Scripture. In the twenty-first century, spiritual seekers are finding their own religious beliefs and the sacred writings that go along with them. Redefined scriptures include the Gnostic Gospels, beliefs attributed to secret societies, clues hidden in ancient art, and Bible codes produced by computer searches. One person's Bible is another person's book of fantasies. How do people of faith and people seeking after faith decide which sacred writings are true?

Chapter 7

SCRIPTURES & SEEKERS

RELIGION & MODERN CULTURE

Elaine Pagels is at the forefront of religious scholarship. She holds a Ph.D. from Harvard University, is professor of religion at Princeton University, and has written three popular books about the development of early Christianity. Her most recent book, *Beyond Belief*, concerns the Gospel of Thomas, the New Testament Canon, and early Christianity. *Beyond Belief* does more than recount history, however. Professor Pagels also gives a candid account of her own spiritual development. She shows how new concepts of scripture can influence one person's spiritual life.

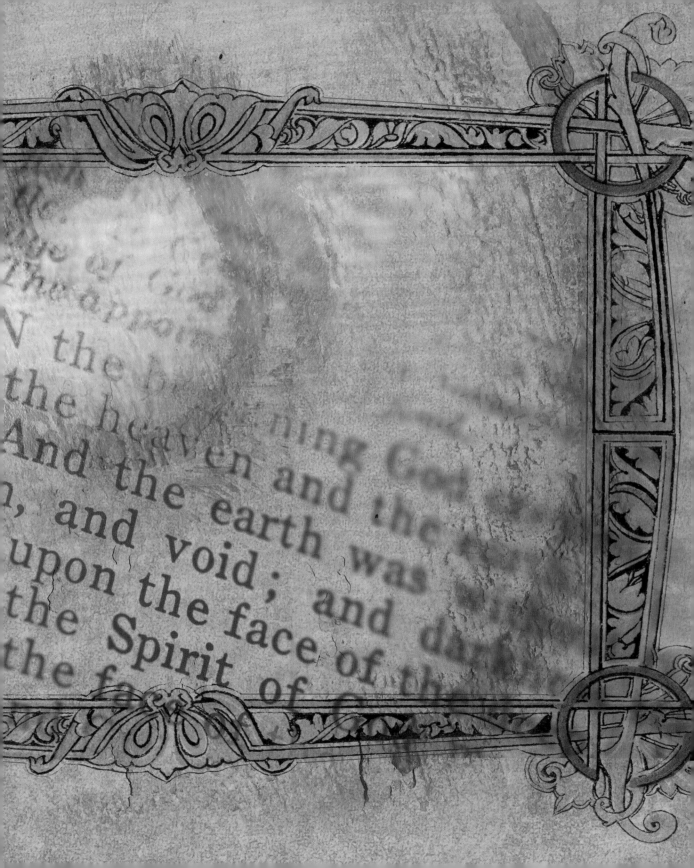

At the start of *Beyond Belief*, Pagels tells how one morning, while jogging, she "stopped into the vaulted stone vestibule of the Church of the Heavenly Rest in New York to catch my breath and warm up." She was experiencing a crisis. She relates how, "Two days before, a team of doctors at Babies Hospital, Columbia Presbyterian Medical Center, had performed a routine checkup on our son, Mark, a year and six months after his successful open-heart surgery." The doctors found a rare lung disease and pronounced that Mark had only a short time to live.

Standing in the back of the church, the worried mother realized that something powerful was taking place in the service. "Here was a place to weep without imposing tears upon a child," a diverse group of people who had found a way "to deal with what we cannot control."

Later in the book, Professor Pagels tells what caused her to question and leave her church as a teenager. At age fourteen, she joined an evangelical Christian church. They provided "the assurance of belonging to the right group, the true 'flock' that alone belonged to God." At age sixteen, a close Jewish friend of Pagels died in a car accident, and her fellow evangelicals declared him eternally damned. She says, "Finding no room for discussion I realized that I was no longer at home in their world and left that church."

She studied Greek in college, hoping to learn more about the New Testament and perhaps come to peace with religious faith. In the Harvard doctoral program, she was astonished to learn of the Nag Hammadi texts: "These discoveries challenged us not only intellectually but—in my case at least—spiritually." She has spent the years since then studying and teaching the Gnostic writings.

She explains later in the book, "When I found that I no longer believed everything I thought Christians were supposed to believe, I asked myself, why not just leave Christianity—and religion—behind, as so many others have done?" Yet something drew her to spiritual belief. Studying the Gospel of Thomas and other texts, Elaine Pagels became convinced that early Christianity was not a "one way" religion, but

rather a movement with great diversity. She found Gnostic texts that emphasize the nature of God within humanity, and urge believers to look inside themselves and find their own religious truth. Pagels does not regard the Gnostic Gospels the way that evangelicals regard the New Testament—as a source of absolute truth. For Pagels, the diversity of Gnostic texts proves there is room in Christianity for a broad variety of beliefs and opinions. The existence of the Nag Hammadi books helped this Princeton professor reconnect with a worshipping community and find strength for her family at a difficult time.

LEE STROBEL: A JOURNALIST'S PERSONAL INVESTIGATION OF THE EVIDENCE FOR JESUS

Lee Strobel recalls the exact moment and place he lost faith in God. He says in an interview: "I was 14 years old. I was a freshman at Prospect High School in suburban Chicago. I was on the third floor, northwest corner of the building, second row from the window, third seat from the back when I heard the evidence that for the first time plunged me into atheism." As long as he could remember, Lee was a careful thinker. He says:

> A lot of people don't give much thought to what they believe and it's easy for them to hold what often are two conflicting ideas in their head at the same time. My background is in journalism and law, and those are two areas that cater to intellectual processes and also to responding to evidence. And so, when I saw the evidence that God was unnecessary, I jettisoned God.

RELIGION & MODERN CULTURE

"As someone educated in journalism and law, I was trained to respond to the facts, wherever they lead. For me, the data demonstrated convincingly that Jesus is the Son of God."

—Lee Strobel

After that, Lee Strobel served as the legal editor of the *Chicago Tribune*. He was a spiritual skeptic until 1981, when he became an evangelical Christian. After that, he became teaching pastor at Willow Creek Community Church in Illinois. He went on to write eleven books, including the best-selling *The Case for Christ*. Currently, he hosts the television talk show *Faith Under Fire*. How did Lee Strobel the atheist become an evangelical Christian?

While Strobel was legal editor for the *Chicago Tribune*, his wife became an evangelical Christian, and that change prompted him to investigate the Gospel documents and their claims about Christ. As an investigative journalist, Strobel knew how important it was to look very carefully at every piece of evidence in a case. He had firsthand experience with cases that seemed "open and shut" but changed dramatically when evidence was reexamined. Therefore, Strobel looked at the New Testament scriptures very carefully.

He also interviewed experts and asked them questions. "Can the biographies of Jesus be trusted? Do the biographies of Jesus stand up to scrutiny? Were Jesus' biographies reliably preserved?" Lee Strobel recorded his research and results in painstaking detail in *The Case for Christ*. Strobel says at the book's conclusion:

After a personal investigation that spanned more than six hundred days and countless hours, my own verdict is the case for Christ was clear. . . . As someone educated in journalism and law, I was trained to respond to the facts, wherever they lead. For me, the data demonstrated convincingly that Jesus is the Son of God.

SCRIPTURES FOR THE TWENTY-FIRST CENTURY

In the New Testament book the Acts of the Apostles, the author says the people of Beroea were "more fair-minded than those in Thessalonica, for they . . . examined the Scriptures daily to determine whether these things were so." In the twenty-first century, there are even more scriptures to examine and more spiritual choices to make as a result. People are searching a variety of sources for religious truth—the New Testament Gospels, the Gospel of Thomas, *The Da Vinci Code*, the Bible code, and so on.

Curiously, while people may question traditional definitions of scripture, few are questioning the concept of scripture itself. According to some, the popularity of *The Da Vinci Code* reflects a sort of "reverse fundamentalism." The novel questions traditional religion, but it does so in the traditional way—by appealing to a different set of ancient scriptures and declaring they are absolute truth.

People of faith may examine the same documents and arrive at differing conclusions. Yet today's spiritual seekers communicate a common need. More than 3,000 years after the Jewish people first began to revere sacred writings, today's religious believers continue to place their faith in books they esteem as the written words of God.

FURTHER READING

Abanes, Richard. *The Truth Behind* The Da Vinci Code. Eugene, Ore.: Harvest House, 2004.

Brown, Dan. *The Da Vinci Code.* New York: Doubleday, 2003.

Cahill, Thomas. *Desire of the Everlasting Hills: The World Before and After Jesus.* New York: Doubleday, 1999.

Cox, Simon. *Cracking* The Da Vinci Code: *The Unauthorized Guide to the Facts Behind Dan Brown's Bestselling Novel.* New York: Barnes and Noble, 2004.

Jenkins, Philip. *Hidden Gospels: How the Search for Jesus Lost Its Way.* New York: Oxford University Press, 2001.

Pagels, Elaine. *Beyond Belief: The Secret Gospel of Thomas.* New York: Vintage, 2003.

Robinson, James M., ed. *The Nag Hammadi Library: The Definitive Translation of the Gnostic Gospels Complete in One Volume.* New York: Harper Collins, 1990.

Strobel, Lee. *The Case for Christ: A Journalist's Personal Investigation of the Evidence for Jesus.* Grand Rapids, Mich.: Zondervan, 1998.

Witherington, Ben, III. *The Gospel Code: Novel Claims About Jesus, Mary Magdalene and Da Vinci.* Downers Grove, Ill.: Intervarsity Press, 2004.

FOR MORE INFORMATION

Gospel of Thomas Commentary
www.gospelthomas.com

Gospel of Thomas Web
Resources
www.bardicpress.com/thomas/
resources.htm

Jesus Seminar Forum Homepage
virtualreligion.net/forum/

Official Web Site of Bestselling
Author Dan Brown
www.danbrown.com

Official Web Site of Opus Dei
www.opusdei.org

Opus Dei Awareness Network
www.odan.org

Religious Movements Homepage
religiousmovements.lib.virginia.edu

Templar History
www.templarhistory.com

PICTURE CREDITS

The illustrations in RELIGION AND MODERN CULTURE are photo montages made by Dianne Hodack. They are a combination of her original mixed-media paintings and collages, the photography of Benjamin Stewart, various historical public-domain artwork, and other royalty-free photography collections.

AUTHOR: Kenneth McIntosh is a freelance writer living in Flagstaff Arizona. He lives with his wife, Marsha, and has two children, Jonathan and Eirené. He has a bachelor's degree in English and a master's degree in theology. He is the author of more than a dozen books. These include *The Grail, the Shroud, and Other Religious Relics: Secrets and Ancient Mysteries and Prophecies* and *End-Time Speculations: The Shape of Things to Come.* He formerly spent a decade teaching junior high in inner-city Los Angeles, and another decade serving as an ordained minister. He enjoys hiking, boogie boarding, and vintage Volkswagens.

CONSULTANT: Dr. Marcus J. Borg is the Hundere Distinguished Professor of Religion and Culture in the Philosophy Department at Oregon State University. Dr. Borg is past president of the Anglican Association of Biblical Scholars. Internationally known as a biblical and Jesus scholar, the *New York Times* called him "a leading figure among this generation of Jesus scholars." He is the author of twelve books, which have been translated into eight languages. Among them are *The Heart of Christianity: Rediscovering a Life of Faith* (2003) and *Meeting Jesus Again for the First Time* (1994), the best-selling book by a contemporary Jesus scholar.

CONSULTANT: Dr. Robert K. Johnston is Professor of Theology and Culture at Fuller Theological Seminary in Pasadena, California, having served previously as Provost of North Park University and as a faculty member of Western Kentucky University. The author or editor of thirteen books and twenty-five book chapters (including *The Christian at Play,* 1983; *The Variety of American Evangelicalism,* 1991; *Reel Spirituality: Theology and Film in Dialogue,* 2000; *Life Is Not Work/Work Is Not Life: Simple Reminders for Finding Balance in a 24/7 World,* 2000; *Finding God in the Movies: 33 Films of Reel Faith,* 2004; and *Useless Beauty: Ecclesiastes Through the Lens of Contemporary Film,* 2004), Johnston is the immediate past president of the American Theological Society, an ordained Protestant minister, and an avid bodysurfer.